D0267935

FOOTBALL: MY LIFE, MY PASSION

GRAEME SOUNESS

FOOTBALL: MY LIFE, MY PASSION

With Douglas Alexander

HEADLINE

Copyright © 2017 Graeme Souness

Text copyright © 2017 Graeme Souness and Douglas Alexander

The right of Graeme Souness to be identified as the Author of
the Work has been asserted by him in accordance with the
Copyright, Designs and Patents Act 1988.

First published in 2017
by HEADLINE PUBLISHING GROUP

Apart from any use permitted under UK copyright law, this publication may
only be reproduced, stored, or transmitted, in any form, or by any means,
with prior permission in writing of the publishers or, in the case of
reprographic production, in accordance with the terms of licences
issued by the Copyright Licensing Agency.

Every effort has been made to fulfil requirements with regard to
reproducing copyright material. The author and publisher will be
glad to rectify any omissions at the earliest opportunity.

Cataloguing in Publication Data is available from the British Library

Hardback ISBN 978 1 4722 4252 5
Trade paperback ISBN 978 1 4722 42549

Typeset in Bliss by Palimpsest Book Production Ltd,
Falkirk, Stirlingshire

Printed and bound in Great Britain by
CPI Group (UK) Ltd, Croydon CR0 4YY

MIX
Paper from
responsible sources
FSC® C104740
FSC www.fsc.org

Headline's policy is to use papers that are natural, renewable
and recyclable products and made from wood grown in sustainable
forests. The logging and manufacturing processes are expected to
conform to the environmental regulations of the country of origin.

HEADLINE PUBLISHING GROUP
An Hachette UK Company
Carmelite House
50 Victoria Embankment
London EC4Y 0DZ

www.headline.co.uk
www.hachette.co.uk

To my wife Karen, for her patience and understanding during my life in football.

RENFREWSHIRE COUNCIL	
243304921	
Bertrams	01/11/2017
796.334	£20.00
CEN	

CONTENTS

1

LUCKY MAN

I am a very lucky man. I have a work contract with Sky that takes me to my 66th birthday. That means from the age of 15, I will have earned wages out of football over a period of 51 years. It has gone way beyond my initial expectations.

To start with, I was a kid worrying if I'd be good enough to join a professional club. Then the work really starts, where you worry if you will be good enough to get into the first team, although I was less worried than most of my contemporaries on that score. Then it was: Will I win anything? Will I play for my country?

I've played with some fantastic players, who, when they finished playing, it was the end of their football life, other than maybe doing some corporate hospitality work on matchdays. Some of these players were serial winners of European Cups and First Division titles, but that was their sole income. I have gone from playing to managing and then into punditry, so football has certainly been very kind to me.

I love it. I've finished being directly involved in football, but I still get the buzz, without having the baggage to take home after the game if you've lost. That's why I feel so lucky. It has all dropped into place perfectly for me.

I got my first taste of media work way back when I was playing at Liverpool. I did the Brighton–Manchester United FA Cup final at Wembley in 1983, as co-commentator with the great Brian Moore. Then I did the European Cup final in 1985, when Liverpool lost 1–0 to Juventus, with Terry Venables in the studio, and it was a difficult night because we were obviously seeing pictures coming in that weren't being put out on air and showed some pretty harrowing stuff after the tragedy at the Heysel stadium in Brussels in which 39 people, mostly Juventus fans, died.

Next, through my relationship with Richard Keys, who I'd known from when he worked at Radio City in Liverpool when I was a player there, I started doing some work for Sky, although I was always conscious when I was still working in the business as a manager that you are on there talking about other people's teams. That's why I was more comfortable discussing Champions League games than anything else back then.

After I was sacked by Newcastle in February 2006, the media work really took off for me. I decided not to go back to management after group of coaches at Liverpool. It would not be something that they wanted to be part of. Bob didn't do press conferences, let alone the sort of post-match television interviews you see managers doing now.

There was the 'Liverpool mafia', where only one reporter would speak to him and then they would dish out the information to the rest. He kept it to a bare minimum. It certainly wasn't something that Bob, or Joe Fagan after him, enjoyed.

The whole thing is very different today. The managers today are more like public relations men. They don't say anything that's critical of their players. When you listen to a lot of managers now, it's like listening to a politician. A lot of it is talking but saying nothing and trying to spin things. That's obviously media training having an impact more and more.

People say Mauricio Pochettino is a young manager at Tottenham at the age of 45. I got the manager's job at Rangers, one of the biggest clubs in British football, aged 33 and I had zero media training, so I was always going to have problems because I had no idea how that relationship worked. I know they get taught on these management courses today how to deal with that, and I would have greatly benefited from it, if it had been open to me at the time.

Instead, I was learning by my mistakes. Only if you've worked in the west of Scotland can you understand it. There are Celtic supporters in the press who lean more towards Celtic, and Rangers supporters in the press who lean more towards Rangers. Human nature is such that you will like some press guys more than others. It's a balancing act as a manager in that situation, because if you favour one reporter and his newspaper, you make an enemy of the other.

Then, when you become a pundit, you start to look at it from a different angle, see it from the other side. Daft little things, like why are we always tucked in the corner in an executive box they can't sell, when television is putting so much money into football? Why do we get the sandwiches that were made the day before and are curled up at the ends, in many, if not all, of the places we go? That's me with a different head on now as a pundit, rather than as a player or manager.

Most of all, why are players today so uncooperative? They just give the bare minimum when it should be the exact opposite. They should be giving more than we ever did, because they owe more to television than we did.

It's a wonderful time to be a footballer, although there couldn't be a more difficult time to be a manager. I would just like the players to realise that the kind of money and adulation they get today is not because they are great players; it's just a great time to be involved in football and television has a large part to play in that. It's the money from television that funds their lifestyle as much as any other income the football club has, yet it would appear, now that I have been on both sides of it, that they give very little back to television companies in return.

It's always under duress. They have only got so much time to speak, they have press officers saying, 'You have two minutes,' and wanting to know what questions are going to be asked in advance. They give very little back for the kind of input that the television companies are committing to football these days.

The PFA could do a hell of a lot more to make players wake up and smell the roses, and realise why the game is flying at this time. It's not that the product all of a sudden has become that fabulous to watch. It's not that the English game is filled with truly great players like Lionel Messi or Cristiano Ronaldo.

It's because television has given them a platform that has increased everyone's profile, and everyone has benefited from that in the professional game. From the hordes of sports scientists now, to all the other affiliates that are employed by football clubs today. The whole football industry has expanded. It's all television money paying for that.

So my request to the players is: just put a bit more back in, please. Be more appreciative of this glorious period for football and what it can offer you day in and day out.

● ● ●

The Premier League has done the deal with television and Sky pay £11 million per Premier League game now. There are over 100 people at every game from Sky. They are putting a hell of a lot into it, in terms of time, effort and money.

If that means playing on a Friday night or a Monday night or a Sunday afternoon at four o'clock, that's the way it has to be. Football has signed up for it, it's taking the money. Clubs are building their stadiums with that money, buying new players with that money, or building a new training ground with that money. It's the price on the ticket and it's no hardship to the players.

When you see them today on the pitch, covering their mouths in case someone lip-reads what they are saying to each other, things have become a little absurd. Are they really going to be saying anything that dramatic or interesting walking off the pitch at half-time?

They have to accept the way it is. They are earning all this money, they are famous, or at least of interest to people, because they are always on the television. There's extra responsibility that comes with that, though. Apart from the money and glamour that television has brought into the game, the people involved have to be more responsible now. That's the interest there is in football today. In one respect it has never been better, but there's also more scrutiny. You can't have it all ways.

Something I accepted when I was a manager is that the television and the press want you as soon as possible after the game, particularly if it has not gone well for you. They want the raw emotion, they don't want you to sit and have a cup of tea and relax and collect your thoughts for half an hour. They want you instantly. That's not a new thing. It has never been any different. They want you to say things that the following day you wish you hadn't said, but that's always been there.

I am also always aware that on live television, you are only ever one sentence away from never being asked back. As I said, it was Richard Keys who got me started at Sky, but he and Andy Gray lost their jobs with Sky after making condescending remarks off air about Sian Massey-Ellis, the assistant referee, before a Premier League game between Liverpool and Wolves in January 2011.

'Somebody better get down there and explain the offside rule to her,' said Richard.

'Can you believe that? A female linesman. That's exactly why I was saying women don't know the offside rule,' replied Andy.

'Of course they don't . . . the game's gone mad,' added Richard.

I can't condone their comments and don't know the context because I wasn't working that day, but I won't be a hypocrite about it either and swear that I've never said anything off air that would be considered less than politically correct. You turn up in a studio a couple of hours before kick-off, and an hour before you go on air, and you talk about all sorts of things. There are microphones on and things are being recorded without you knowing they are. I am sure if they looked long and hard enough for any of us who are in the studio, we'd all be embarrassed by things we've said.

I am still appreciative to Richard, he introduced me to the business and helped me a great deal in the early days, and Andy is still arguably the best co-commentator out there, although he doesn't do a lot of it today. Where Richard is very good is he spent 25 years with Andy learning the game and has a great memory. You can be doing a show with him and he'll ask you a question and then say, 'Two seasons ago, you didn't say that about such and such a player.' He'll challenge you and I think that makes for interesting television. He has a memory like an elephant and is a true student of the game. He knows everything that's happening, all over the Premier League and beyond.

I prefer being in the studio. I was never as comfortable doing co-commentary. I was thrust straight into co-commentary without any coaching or practice and it's not something I do now. Besides my contract with Sky, I have one with TV3 in Dublin for the Champions League as well as my newspaper column for *The Sunday Times*.

My golden rule in my work is that you have to say what you believe is correct. That may sometimes mean criticising a club or player that you have an affinity with or previously worked with, but you have to call it the way you see it, otherwise it's obvious to the viewer or reader.

I don't like to hear people using the word 'we' when they are talking about their old teams – 'We were good today, we weren't good today.' That irritates slightly. When you are doing this job, you have to be as independent as you possibly can. You are paid to give an opinion honestly, without fear or favour.

While it can be a lot of fun, you also have to remember it's a serious business. What you have to take on board is that when you are saying critical stuff about a particular club, there are supporters who will go home and it will totally ruin their weekend, because their team has not turned up on that day, and been beaten badly. I don't think we can ever trivialise that. You like to think if their team has not done well, you are actually saying what they would like to say in being critical.

Having previously been in the position myself, I fully get that some of the guys in punditry still have one eye on management or getting into coaching and they sometimes back off from the confrontational moments because of that. One of the episodes from my broadcasting career that people remember best was my criticism of Carlos Tevez when he apparently refused to come off the bench and play in Manchester City's Champions League game at Bayern Munich in September 2011.

I was on with Mark Hughes and Dwight Yorke, when Tevez refused to warm up for Roberto Mancini. It was an awkward situation for Mark because he had signed Tevez for City and they shared the same agent, Kia Joorabchian, at the time, while Dwight lived in Alderley Edge and could have bumped into Tevez at any time there. They both felt they had to hold back, whereas I could say what everyone was really thinking: 'He's a disgrace.'

I pointed out that most people start playing football because they love it and a few of us are fortunate enough to eventually be paid to play it, and then there is a smaller group still who are paid an awful lot of money to do so, a group that Tevez definitely belonged to.

The marker I put down on that night was important for football in this country, although it was in the Champions League. We do things differently from most other countries. It's a very successful league we have and we can't have people coming here and introducing standards of behaviour that would not be helpful in the bigger picture. I was saying that not against Tevez, but about standards of conduct we have and must maintain in our football.

I get that there are people who I work with who are still looking to go back into coaching and therefore can't always call it as they really see it. I made up my mind a long time ago that it was a fence that I was prepared to jump. I don't go out of my way to do it, but I will do it.

That's why I thought it was very brave of Gary Neville to move back into coaching and management, when he could have comfortably stayed in television for 25 years and could still do so, now he has returned to it. He could also have taken on far easier jobs than Valencia as his first one.

Valencia regard themselves as just behind Real Madrid and Barcelona in Spain, in terms of being a big club. It's a difficult enough job when that team is going well, but Gary took it on when they were struggling. It was brave, but perhaps foolish on his part.

Then there was the England role for Gary, as Roy Hodgson's assistant for Euro 2012 and 2016 and the 2014 World Cup. He's had two real bloody noses in his short coaching and managerial career so far. Those have just been two high-profile jobs that didn't go well. I've experienced management jobs that didn't go well, but I've also experienced jobs that did go well, where I won things. Fortunately, I tasted the good before the bad.

What that does to your confidence going forward, where there's so much expected of you and it doesn't work out, only Gary can answer long term; there is also the question of whether he ends up going back and having another go.

I thought the England job was a particularly difficult one for him in combination with his broadcasting commitments. On a Sunday afternoon, he could be doing co-commentary of a game England players were playing in and then, a few hours afterwards, he's in a hotel in London with some of the boys he has been critical of. He would have been compromised by that in both environments.

The show with Gary and Jamie Carragher on a Monday night is a good one, they make it very interesting. It has certainly added to Sky's coverage, but it will greatly irritate some in the professional game, where you have guys who have recently finished playing telling them where they are going wrong. No-one likes to be criticised in public and, of course, we highlight things then repeat it, so it's like rubbing their noses in it.

The pundits, meanwhile, have to accept that's their job, that they are on there to do that, stick their neck out and take any flak that comes their way as a consequence. It's harder for them because they have to criticise people they have maybe played against, because they are not as long out of the game as I am.

I am conscious that I am working with guys who are considerably younger than me, coming from a completely different generation, but the game doesn't change. You have to do the same things to win games and if you make certain mistakes you will still lose games. The winning attitude doesn't change and it's not a generation thing that we sometimes disagree with each other. It's a football thing. Some people don't work out that less is more; that the more you say, the less you are getting your message across.

The new lads coming in have improved it again. They look very good on screen, they are all opinionated and they have brought it up to another level. Thierry Henry has yet to make the jump across the fence. The others have jumped it several times. Thierry's take on the game, his analysis of situations, is nine times out of 10 the same as I see it, but he doesn't want to be over-critical because I think he will be a manager in the Premier League one day and I get that.

I like Glenn Hoddle, on and off the screen. I've also worked with Gianluca Vialli, my old Sampdoria teammate, a couple of times and he's very intelligent. I like listening to his take on things.

In Ireland, I was the voice of reason when I worked with Eamon Dunphy, the broadcaster and former footballer, for RTE. Well, sort of. I enjoyed working with him there and with Johnny Giles, the former Leeds and Republic of Ireland midfielder, who is a very wise old football man.

Another guy I have enjoyed working with and spending time off screen with is Neil Lennon. Despite being former managers of Rangers and Celtic, we get on very well and find we agree on most things.

● ● ●

People often complain there's too much football on television now, but it boils down to one thing: if the public didn't want it, it wouldn't be there. The public demand it and are prepared to pay for it. It's what they want to watch.

The coverage is fabulous. I firmly believe it has brought everyone that reports on football, from the written journalists to radio and other television companies, to a new level. At Sky, we've set the standards for them all to match. Not just the pundits, but the way it is actually presented and how it is put together.

For kids, there will always be time to play football. You are not going to learn something new every day listening to us, and the kid who really wants to be a player will always make time to play football as well as watch it.

I actually think if there had been more coverage in my childhood, I would have been a better player because of it. You are watching and learning a lot more, understanding a lot more. By watching the top players and seeing how they deal with different situations, you would also be able to work out people's weaknesses as well. We microscope everything, don't we? It shows people's failings as well as their positives.

It has also encouraged debate and opinion on football, although there are upsides and downsides to that. At 30, as captain of Liverpool and Scotland, having won what I'd won, I could not offer an opinion in a team meeting to challenge the wisdom of men like Bob Paisley, Joe Fagan and Ronnie Moran. I wouldn't have dared challenge them.

Today, because of what we've done, there's so much analysis of football that a young 20-year-old, who has played 10 times in the first-team, has an opinion. If you go into a dressing room now, the young boys who have hardly kicked a ball will have an opinion and they will voice it.

I find that, generally, I get a good reaction to my television work. British people like pundits who speak their minds. I accept that if you are working at Chelsea, for argument's sake, and you have been critical of a couple of their players, you can't shy away from that and you have to be able to defend your opinion if you are challenged by a supporter at Stamford Bridge or someone from the club.

At Manchester United, there's always the thing of, 'He's anti-United because he used to play for and manage Liverpool', but it's not the case. I try to be fair all the time and people seem to get that, because I don't get a great deal of grief anywhere really. I don't have any issues with that at all.

The best game I have covered was when Manchester City won the Premier League in 2012, for the first time in 44 years, through Sergio Aguero's goal five minutes into stoppage-time against Queens Park Rangers, the last kick of the ball in the season. We were on the pitch afterwards, broadcasting from there, and it took me back to when I'd won something myself as a player or manager. That was a special day.

BT have the Champions League rights in Britain now, but, with Sky, we had some fabulous nights because they used to do the group stages from Isleworth and then we would go to the quarter-finals, if there was an interesting one, the semi-finals and final. We had some memorable trips to the great stadiums in Europe, like the Allianz Arena in Munich, Camp Nou in Barcelona and the Bernabeu in Madrid. They were all on the semi-final hit-list most years.

The Bernabeu was the best for me. The Munich stadium has all the facilities, but the Bernabeu stands out as an experience overall. Maybe because of what's in your head when you go there, at my age anyway, it's such a special place with the history behind it. At Camp Nou, in contrast, you are literally in the Gods in the media area and the players look like little table football figures. It's not a great place to watch football.

Having said that, we did the semi-final at the Bernabeu in 2015, when Juventus knocked Real Madrid out, and it wasn't the greatest viewpoint that Thierry Henry, Jamie Redknapp and I had there either.

We were pitch-side beforehand and then we were ushered off it at the start of the game, after we had done our bit, to a little cubby-hole underneath the stadium, where the groundsman sat with his coffee and sandwiches. That was where we watched the game from, the smallest, pokiest little space. It was a cupboard. There we were, all sitting on each other's knees, watching the semi-final of the Champions League on a television screen.

I believe we are still just scratching the surface of the relationship between football and television. For example, the Chinese government is funding the development of football there, which means for the next 20 years it's only going to get bigger, so the Premier League will be of more value when it comes to television rights in China and Asia in general.

There are 743 million people living in Europe, but over a billion live in India and over a billion in China. All the big teams go out that way in pre-season to build up their brands. It's an enormous market that's still relatively untapped. In the television world, the same will apply.

But how do you control illegal streaming? If people can watch it and are no longer tied to Sky or BT, if they can pull it down from a satellite and not pay for it, they will do that. Take that further forward and will Sky or BT be able to keep bidding for the TV rights at the levels they are now, because if fans can see a stream for free in the UK, they can stream it in China and India as well?

Personally, I will do my television work as long as people want me to, because I get a buzz out of it. Psychologically, because I am not working every day, as I was in football management, it's good for me, too.

I am very lucky. To think that I have had the career that football has given me and it's now come to this, where I don't work every weekend and, when I do, I get to go to some marvellous stadiums, see some great games of football and catch up with some old adversaries and friends. I still get a football buzz, a football fix, and a clothes allowance, too. It's fantastic. I'm so blessed.

GETTING STARTED

Sometimes you need to take one step back to move two steps forward in football. That was the story of my playing career, certainly the start of it, where I grew impatient at not being given a first-team chance at Tottenham and moved to Middlesbrough. I was a late developer physically, while mentally I turned from a boy into a man under the demanding management of Jack Charlton as Middlesbrough won the Second Division title in 1974.

I suspect that lots of kids like me are lost to football these days. I look at the pressure to remain in the Premier League, the pressure to win things at the big clubs and qualify for the Champions League, or even that each position higher you finish in the league table is worth an extra £2 million – that's why it's harder for kids today to break through, because managers often just can't afford to give them their chance.

Alex Ferguson would often play his Manchester United kids in the League Cup, including the ones he knew were not good enough going forward. He would put them in the shop window, because the League Cup didn't matter compared to the league and Europe, and he knew he was increasing their transfer values by doing that. United would then sell players for big money because they were 'first-team' players, but they were only first-team players in the League Cup.

Managers are under so much pressure now not to play their young players in Premier League games. If you are down near the bottom, it's all about survival. If you are near the top, it's about getting into the Champions League or having a chance of winning the league, so young players tend to miss out because they are an unknown quantity. That's how the game has gone.

Then you have the influx of foreigners. With the money that's now in the English game, coming here is very attractive to all the top players. When I played in Italy, the national manager was always complaining that there were no central midfielders coming through, because at the time all the clubs in Italy wanted their *registas*, the deep-lying playmakers, or their strikers from abroad. They were not developing their own talent in those key positions, because they had all been filled by the foreigners.

I guess, in my era, the Scots, Irish and Welsh were the players who did that in England. At Liverpool, when Kenny Dalglish, Alan Hansen and I occupied positions down the spine of the team, we were stopping an England prospect from picking up the invaluable experience we did in our successful European campaigns. In those days, there was a steady stream of Scottish talent pouring into England that has, sadly, since dried up.

I was part of that tradition. My own childhood in Edinburgh was an extremely happy one that equipped me with the skills I needed to succeed in football and in life. It gave me a sense of security that bred the self-confidence that helped me make it over the various hurdles you need to clear to become a professional then an international footballer. It was also a time where I spent many hours perfecting my technique, which is perhaps what stopped happening in Scotland in the generations that followed my own.

I was brought up in a prefab house that backed onto a school playing field, and I always had someone to play with because I had two older brothers, Billy and Gordon. Like World Cups, the Souness sons arrived every four years. Gordon is four years older than Billy, who is four years older than me. I still speak to them regularly, but I'm my own man and always have been.

I've never relied on them throughout my life. I was encouraged to stand on my own two feet by them as much as by my parents, Elizabeth and James. It was seldom a case of, 'I'll get my big brothers to fight my battles', and there were a few of them as I moved from Broomhouse Primary to Carrickvale Secondary. They would have kicked me up the backside if I had gone down that road. That was the way we were brought up.

The only time I can ever recall playing the big-brother card was after I knew Tottenham wanted me. Charlie Faulkner, their chief scout, had been in touch to let me know that was the case. The school went on a day trip to Hillend Ski Centre in Edinburgh and when I told the instructor that I didn't want to ski in case I injured myself and lost out on my chance at White Hart Lane, he pulled me into a room and pushed me against some ski poles. Only under that extreme provocation did I finally snap and ask him how he would get on against someone his own age.

My mother had a part-time job in the government offices, which were a mile from where we lived, and my father was a glazier. My mother handed out the discipline. I can never remember my father disciplining me, maybe because he was out working all the time. My mother would be the one and, if I ran away, my brothers would catch me and give it to me. My parents can say they did a very good job of bringing up three boys.

Mum would often say to me, 'Wherever you'll be, there will never be a dull moment.' She also said, 'You can never sit down.' She was right on both counts. That's the way I am. I can never sit still; I always have to be doing something. I find it hard to sit down and watch television. It has to really grab my attention. I even find it hard to sit down and watch 90 minutes of football. I have ants in my pants, as they say in Scotland, and as a youngster that would sometimes get me into mischief. Mum knew if I had been fighting or was in trouble of some kind. She just had that mother's sixth sense.

Dad was a decent player, a left-winger, who broke his leg playing football just before his regiment were due be shipped out to the Second World War. The vast majority of them didn't come back, so he was lucky. Mum had already lost a previous boyfriend, who was on board HMS *Hood* when it was sunk by the German battleship *Bismarck* in May 1941, so she didn't need any more heartbreak from the war.

Dad was a gently-spoken, mild and a very popular man. Mum was a little more outspoken, but she wasn't aggressive either. Both my parents were quite mild-mannered. If I was playing in a big game on a Saturday, Dad would give me a massage on the Friday night and clean my boots. He must have seen something in me. I was always the bairn of the family, and I still am.

Mum used to make me macaroni cheese on a Saturday at lunchtime. I'd play for the schools in the morning and for Tynecastle Boys Club in the afternoon, so it gave me energy for the second game of the day. My first medal came around the age of seven. I played in a cup final for my primary school, Billy was in goals for that game, so all the other players would have been four years older than me, and we won. I was a left-winger then because I was so small compared to the rest.

For some reason that I've never got to the bottom of, I went to Broomhouse Primary rather than Stenhouse, which was closer to where we lived. No sooner had I established myself there than it was time for secondary school. I was the only kid from Broomhouse that went to Carrickvale. The rest went to another school nearby called Forrester's.

I'd played for Edinburgh schools by that stage, so I came with a bit of a reputation and had to establish myself again. I was joining Carrickvale as Billy was leaving, and I wasn't going with any of my mates because they had all gone somewhere else, but there was no sense of, 'I am out of my depth here', because of my personality. I just dealt with it, it wasn't an issue.

That was something that stood me in good stead throughout my football career. I was never fazed by moving to a new club or dressing room, even one as successful as Liverpool's. I always felt I belonged in any company.

I got into a few scrapes in my childhood, however, that could have put my career in jeopardy. I was lucky to escape serious injury when I fell off my school roof one day. It was the annexe adjacent to my house that was built as a corrugated structure, like the prefabs. It was supposed to be a temporary build after the war, but was there for a very long time. You could climb up on the roof and I ended up falling off it and broke my arm.

Another time, our next-door neighbour Norman and I were throwing a pickaxe in the garden when I actually hit him with it by accident. It glanced off his head, which was quite a scary moment for him. I also broke my collarbone at school: I was messing around with someone on my shoulders and, as I fell, he fell on top of me.

One summer, I went with a friend and his family on holiday to Butlin's and won the Body Beautiful competition there. The prize was a week's holiday the following year, so my mum and dad had to save up to take me. I put them under some pressure there.

Football was a relatively safe pastime in comparison to some of my antics. When I look back, it certainly helped my technique that I used to spend hours kicking a ball against a wire fence at school. The ball would come back at you at different heights and sort of spring back at you as well. I used to love half-volleying the ball, and I was good at it when I later became a professional. My touch was developed there more than anywhere else, just out in the back garden, against that fence round the annexe of my secondary school.

I never really had heroes. I always get asked, 'Who did you model your game on?', but I never really did that. For me, it was always about playing the game. At the time, there were talented guys around like Willie Henderson at Rangers and Jimmy Johnstone at Celtic, but I was always too busy playing.

● ● ●

A pivotal point in my career was representing Scotland Schoolboys against England at White Hart Lane. The late, great Dave Mackay had broken his leg, for the second time, and came to watch because he noticed in the programme I was a kid from Carrickvale, the same school he went to. It was then that I first came to Tottenham's attention.

Dave Mackay had been rammed down my throat from the age of 12, until the age of 19 when I left Tottenham. Every time I did something wrong at school, Mackay was mentioned. For some reason, there were a couple of medals Mackay had won at Carrickvale that were still on the mantelpiece in the headmaster's office. That's what I remember and I was always told, 'You'll never be as good as him.'

Bill Nicholson, Tottenham's double-winning manager, whenever he put a training session on, would also refer to Mackay, saying, 'Dave Mackay would do it this way', so I was flattered when he compared me to Mackay early in my career at Tottenham.

The praise perhaps went to my head when I used to pester him to play me ahead of the likes of Martin Peters, a World Cup winner in 1966, and Alan Mullery, who was England's captain and in the team when they defended their title in Mexico four years later.

'I really think this boy will be another Mackay,' Bill said of me when I was 17. 'For his age, he has wonderful control. In one match, two came at him. He went one way, then the other. He didn't touch the ball but he beat both men and was off, through the gap.'

Mackay must have been some player because if you speak to anyone from that era at Tottenham, they talk about him in such glowing terms. It wasn't about John White or Danny Blanchflower, his fellow midfielders. He was the main man by a country mile. He was, in their eyes, the best.

I got inducted into the English Football Hall of Fame in 2007 and, appropriately, it was Dave that gave me my plaque. I told him I was fed up of hearing his name and we had a laugh about it. When I went to Tottenham as a young boy, I remember one pre-season game where he put his arm round me in front of all the big first-team guys and the other apprentices and said, 'We Carrickvale boys have to stick together among the English.' You can imagine how proud it made me feel.

That day I played for Scotland Schoolboys, we beat England at White Hart Lane and then Wales in Cardiff before I had a prima donna moment that I am still not proud of, but shows how headstrong I was back then. After the win over Wales, there was a training get-together back in Scotland. John Robertson, who also went on to be a full international and played with me at two World Cups, in 1978 and 1982, was there and always reminds me that they gave me a bib with a number 10 and I said, 'I only wear number 4.'

Quite rightly, they said, 'If you don't want this, off you go.' So off I went and never played again. They lost to England the second time without me, though.

On another occasion, I was meant to be playing for Edinburgh Schools against Liverpool Schools at Goodison Park. It was non-stop rain, though, and it was called off, so Eric Carruthers, my pal, who also played for Edinburgh schools, and I went to Anfield and Goodison for a look round instead. I can remember being shown the pitches and I also remember there were two guys at Anfield in white coats cleaning boots and I always wondered afterwards if one of them was Bob Paisley or Joe Fagan, who would later manage me.

Eric later went to Hearts. He had as much ability as me, but perhaps didn't have the determination and dedication I had to go with it. After Hearts, he went to Derby, then drifted out of it and went to play in Australia. We were the two young lads who would have had most chance of making it at that time from the Edinburgh Schools team and were good friends.

I also trained with Celtic on midweek nights for a while. I came out of Parkhead one night and was waiting for the bus to take me into George Square, where I would catch the train back to Edinburgh from Queen Street station, with a fellow young hopeful when this guy came along and started mouthing off at us. When we answered back, he pulled out this sword. I was never renowned for my pace, but showed a bit of it that night to get back up to Parkhead as fast as I could.

After that, Jim Craig, Celtic's right-back when they won the European Cup in 1967, who was also a dentist and trained part-time, used to drive us into Queen Street. I'd buy my fish and chips there and sit on the train on the way back to Edinburgh eating them. Those were happy days.

I also had a trial for West Bromwich Albion at Whitley Bay in the winter. We played in constant sleet and it was blowing a gale, too. My short-sleeved shirt didn't provide much protection, although I greatly enjoyed my first prawn cocktail during that trip.

The offers of professional contracts then started to come in. I got an offer to join West Bromwich, then one to go to Wolves, who were a big club at the time with some serious history behind them, and Tottenham.

I met the Rangers manager, Davie White, with my father and could have gone there. I had also been training at Celtic, and they said they would be in touch in the summer, but we never heard back from them. That would have been ironic, given what would come later, with me managing Rangers. Celtic had just won the European Cup and were one of the best teams in Europe at the time, but I had my heart set on going to England.

I just fancied it more. I'd lived with my grandmother since I was 12 to keep her company and that gave me my independence early in life. I don't know if it was the bigger stage that captured my imagination or that, when I played at Tottenham for Scotland Schoolboys, it was a lovely sunny day. Maybe I fancied living in London, or it was a combination of all those things. They were a glamorous team and there was that Dave Mackay connection, too.

I'd had a seamless schoolboy career, progressing from Edinburgh Schools at primary level, then Scottish Schools at Under-15, then I signed for Tottenham and we won the prestigious FA Youth Cup. We played Coventry City in the final over two legs and I certainly made an impact. We won the first game 1–0 and I scored the goal. Then we went up there, lost 1–0, and I got booked. We tossed a coin for the third game and it was up there again, 2–2, and I was sent off.

The fourth game was back at White Hart Lane. We won 1–0, I scored the goal again, but the FA said I couldn't get a winner's medal because I'd been sent off in the third game. I got my £12 win bonus, but was fined £10, so I didn't exactly cash in our success. I never got the medal either. Bill Nicholson said he would get one specially made for me, but it never appeared.

I was sent off for throwing a punch at Dennis Mortimer, who went on to be Aston Villa's captain when they won the European Cup in 1982, yet at that time I was a different kind of player than I was during my peak years. I didn't fill out physically until after I left Tottenham, as I remember it. I was always an aggressive player, but I was a skilful, tricky midfielder back then, more of a dribbler and a ball player. Then I became a lot more powerful at 20, it seemed to happen overnight for me, and I became strong and developed into a holding midfield player.

We had a fabulous youth team. Ray Clarke, who went on to play for Ajax and later became a top scout for several clubs, was the centre-forward who got all the goals. Phil Holder was a tough little midfielder, a really good footballer. Mick Flanagan, the winger who later went to Charlton, was a good player, as was Barry Daines, the goalkeeper. At the back, Bob Almond later ended up in the New Zealand team when I played against them at the 1982 World Cup in Spain for Scotland.

Steve Perryman was 18 months older than me and he got into the first team early. Steve became a man before the rest of us. He was aggressive and could get around the park. I suppose I felt I had more technique than him, but he was in front of me in terms of maturity and I could later understand and accept why he made it into the first team before me.

Part of my problem and why I became so frustrated was that Bill Nicholson never communicated a great deal. If only someone had said to me at the time, 'We think you have got a chance, just be patient', but no-one ever told me that. It was a hard school. Eddie Baily, Bill's assistant, was a real character, a bit of a sergeant-major type, but funny with it. He was always on my back and we had a few rows, but looking back now I appreciate it was all being done to help me make it.

The youth coach, Pat Welton, who was in charge of us, was always encouraging, but neither Bill Nicholson nor Eddie ever said we were in their future plans for the first team. I used to knock on Bill's door on a regular basis when the teamsheet would go up on a Friday, saying, 'Why am I not in the team? I feel I'm ready for it.'

The closest I came to feeling part of that scene was through my fellow Scots. Alan Gilzean was another who was fabulous, great to me. There were only the two of us Scots, as Dave Mackay left shortly after I signed.

Of course, I was just a boy, but Gilly made a fuss of me and I never forgot that. His mantra was that you could either play or you couldn't, and no amount of coaching would change that. He had the skill to back that up. Martin Chivers, his striking partner, was another who made me feel welcome when he didn't have to.

You look back now and have this lasting impression in your head of the friendly senior professionals, and the not-so-friendly ones who I won't name. Pat Jennings was another I liked a lot. I still see Pat now because the television studios at White Hart Lane are next to the Pat Jennings Lounge. Phil Beal, the centre-back, is somebody else who I enjoy catching up with when I work there. The last time I saw him, he was still talking about Dave Mackay.

Back in the day, you had to knock on the first-team's dressing room door before you went in. Now all that has long gone in football, but what I learnt at Tottenham, I learnt from the senior pros, by watching how they behaved and trained. I also became aware of the lifestyle that being a successful footballer could offer me. That's why I have always maintained, throughout my career as a player and manager, that the senior pros set and maintain the standards at a club.

Yet, with me, it was taking a while for that message to sink in. After I returned home to Scotland one summer, Bill became convinced that I was looking for a move back there permanently and he was determined that would not happen.

It wasn't another club that had caught my eye, but Julie Ingram, a pretty, dark-haired civil servant. That romance, added to my frustration at not making the first team at Tottenham, led to homesickness, and I decided I'd had enough of London and headed back to Edinburgh.

Today you can flick on the TV and have access to several hundred channels. In my day, there were two channels in black and white and after 10pm there was nothing on, so it was a case of getting out and entertaining yourself. I remember my mum saying to me when I was 14, 'You seem to have lost interest in football, son', and that resonated with me. It was maybe the girls starting to kick in a bit.

I'd run away once before, with no money and no train ticket. I poured my heart out to a kind stranger, who took pity on me and paid my fare and I, of course, kept my promise of posting the money back to them afterwards. I was back so quickly that time that nothing more was said, but this time it was in all the papers and the club were left with no alternative but to suspend me and insist I would be held to my contract, which still had two years to run.

It became a far bigger fuss than I'd anticipated. The late Tam Dalyell, then MP for West Lothian, even raised it in the House of Commons, asking if Tottenham had the right to deprive a minor of following his chosen profession simply because he was homesick. Danny Blanchflower, a former Tottenham captain, came to see me at my parents' home and wrote a sympathetic article for the *Sunday Express* afterwards. After the interview, Danny gave me a coaching lesson in the front room between the sofa and the chairs. I was certainly making waves in my mid-teens.

I tried a couple of jobs out of football without much success. I quickly realised that I wasn't cut out for the removals business when I helped Gerry Ritchie, a mate, carry a piano up three flights of stairs. That, apart from helping load and unload a fruit lorry, was my only day's work outside of football and it made me more receptive to a return to Tottenham.

The chance for a truce came when they came north to play Dunfermline and Bill wrote to Mum and Dad asking them to take me to the game to discuss the stand-off, which had run to seven weeks by then. It was an awkward meeting, as Bill wasn't the greatest in that sort of situation, and afterwards I felt the club had had their fill of me. Only once, as a substitute for a Uefa Cup tie in Iceland, did I make it onto the pitch as a first-team player.

These days, young prospects are farmed out on loan as part of their development. For example, Harry Kane went to Leyton Orient, Millwall, Norwich and Leicester before making his breakthrough at Tottenham and then establishing himself as the main man in Mauricio Pochettino's team.

My loan spell didn't lead to such prominence, but was more exotic and I must admit a lot of fun at the time. In the summer of 1972, I was packed off to Canada with Mick Dillon, my pal at Tottenham, to play for Montreal Olympique in the North American Soccer League. The football wasn't great, but I loved the experience and I enjoyed myself so much that I put on a stone in the first month, mainly due to eating too many late-night burgers after evenings of drunken debauchery.

I played 10 games and travelled all over America and Canada for them, which was fabulous for a 19-year-old lad, really exciting. You were also getting a little taste of being in someone's first team. We were a motley crew, but I must have been doing quite well there because an agent approached me and asked me if I would be interested in going to play in Mexico.

I said of course I would be, although I don't know if Tottenham would have let me go or not. It was an adventure. I was in Canada, so next stop Mexico was how I saw it, but when the coach of the Mexican club came to watch me at the Dallas Cowboys stadium, indoors on an artificial pitch, I failed to impress him. I missed a penalty and was also sent off.

We had six of us sharing a one-bedroom flat at one point, which made things a little chaotic at times and, although we usually eased off the night before a game, it was one big round of parties. We were due to fly back to London straight after our final game, so naturally we had our farewell party beforehand. Being under the influence of something is probably why I scored a rare goal with my head in that game.

Going back to the reserves at Tottenham at the end of September was a major comedown from our heady three months in Montreal, although it was probably for the best in terms of my career, as there were too many distractions in Canada and zero discipline. It proved only a short return to Tottenham, as the end of my time there came at Christmas in 1972.

I was back in Edinburgh again for the festive season and was in a local sports shop when a call came from my brother Billy to say Tottenham had called the family home and said they had agreed a fee for me to go to Middlesbrough. I said, 'Well, I'll go and speak to them then', because I knew I wasn't wanted at White Hart Lane.

My attitude was that if Middlesbrough were prepared to pay money for me and Tottenham were prepared to let me go, enough said, so I went there, signed for them and it became the club where I did a lot of overdue growing up.

● ● ●

I ended up at Middlesbrough because Harold Shepherdson, who was Alf Ramsey's trainer with England, had the same role at Ayresome Park under Stan Anderson, the manager who signed me. Martin Peters, Martin Chivers and Alan Mullery had recommended me to Harold while on England duty.

I was told by Bill Nicholson that I could also have gone to Millwall and Charlton, they both wanted to buy me, but he wanted to sell me to a club as far from Tottenham and London as he possibly could. He nearly got his wish. There was only Sunderland and Newcastle further away in England.

I like to think I was his biggest mistake, in terms of letting people go, and that I proved that during the remainder of my playing career. I went on to win promotion with Middlesbrough to the First Division in 1974, while Tottenham were relegated in 1977, and then I went on to all my success at Liverpool.

I remember one First Division match in March 1975, when I scored twice against my former club in a 3–0 win over them at Ayresome Park. One of the goals is a particularly clear memory, as I went through and rounded Pat Jennings to score in front of the home fans.

Yet I retain a great fondness for both clubs and still like to see them doing well. The current Tottenham are a very different team: for the first time since I started my career as a professional footballer there, they appear to be genuine title contenders. They have a bit of something about them and they look like they could win the Premier League in the next few years. I hope they can pull it off.

Similarly, I don't want Middlesbrough to go on being a yo-yo club. I want them to get into the Premier League and stay there. Steve Gibson deserves that because he gives his managers a bit of time, there's no knee-jerk reaction. He has been a good chairman, arguably the best of the modern era. I've never had the chance to go back to either club as manager, though. I obviously left a good impression!

Middlesbrough were in the Second Division when I signed for them. Soon afterwards, we lost away to Plymouth Argyle in the FA Cup and Stan Anderson, who had signed me, resigned shortly after that. Harold Shepherdson took over as caretaker for a while before the man who would finally get my career going arrived in May 1973. I had just turned 20 and badly needed the strict discipline that Jack Charlton provided.

Quite what he made of me when we first met, I dread to think. I had been away on a summer adventure, driving from Edinburgh to Greece and back again, and returned with bags under my eyes and inches on my waist. Jack was not impressed and he told me straight, 'There are two doors for you: you can go and be a player and have a career, or you can be like so many other talented young men and do nothing with it.' He perhaps didn't put it quite as politely as that.

Nevertheless, I quickly responded to his straightforward approach. He definitely brought the best out of me and made me grow up in terms of being tougher on the football pitch. 'If we are winning 3–0, make it 4–0,' he would tell us.

It was the first time I learnt that when you are on top of a team and have your foot on their throat, you keep them there and don't let them up. That was the attitude. Jack was quite ruthless. He wanted you to be aggressive and I was ready for all that because I was becoming stronger physically. I was becoming a man.

It was Jack's way or the highway. I soon sussed that out, but some didn't and were moved on ruthlessly by him. He left most of the training to Ian McFarlane, his assistant, and Jimmy Greenhalgh, his coach, between games, while he headed for Scotland to do some fishing or hunting, his two great loves.

He certainly came to life on matchdays, though, particularly if we weren't performing. One day we had to duck for cover when he hurled a crate of lemonade across the dressing room at us.

It was Jack who moulded me into a more aggressive midfielder and added a bit of cynicism, too, although that had always been there. I remember playing boys' football and rattling into someone and a parent was ready to run on to take revenge before Gordon, my eldest brother, squared up to him on the side of the pitch. That aggression was always within me.

I got on really well with Jack. He was a bit like Jock Stein in many ways. He was severe on me, but I think that was because he could see someone who had a chance of doing something.

He would take the mickey out of me, a bit like Jock did, slagging off my gear or my hair. I used to turn up with the shampoo, the conditioner and the hairdryer and Jack would laugh at that. I'd be sitting in the bath after games and Jack would say, 'Shampoo? I've never washed my hair in my life', and he would be standing there with about 10 strands coming out of the top of his head and all the lads were finding it hard not to snigger. He used carbolic soap instead. 'This is what I used, son, I never used shampoo on my head,' he'd say.

I also learnt a lot from Bobby Murdoch, who had won the European Cup with Celtic in 1967, because he had been around the block and done everything in the game. Bobby was a good passer of the ball, he had every club in his bag in that respect, but certainly wasn't the most mobile by the time he came to Middlesbrough. He was a lovely football player and somebody that could look after himself, and that rubbed off on me.

We won the Second Division in Jack's first season by 15 points, losing only four of 42 games. We were the best team by a distance. We had a fairly direct, aggressive approach and steamrollered teams.

John Hickton and David Mills, our strikers, didn't look to come short and get involved in anything. It was all about turning the opposition and then pushing in behind them. They were two willing runners. John was strong and aggressive, a big, old-fashioned English centre-forward, while Millsy was very quick. The pair were a real handful for most teams.

I was happier on the pitch and off it, too, where Phoebe Haigh, the landlady at my digs, was like a second mother to me. She was an incredible woman. She had two daughters and I was like the son she'd never had in the way she looked after me. There was a proper cooked meal every night. If I was going for a night out, she would make me have a glass of milk before I went, and when I came back at two in the morning, probably with too much alcohol on board, I had a freshly-made sandwich covered in polythene with a bit of homemade coffee or chocolate cake waiting for me.

I can't emphasise enough how good Phoebe was for me. Her daughters were Beryl and June and I became like their brother. Beryl and I were the same age and June was a bit younger. Beryl was sensible, but I kept an eye out for June because she was the wild one.

Jack established us in the First Division and turned me into an international player, one that Liverpool were prepared to pay a then record fee between English clubs of £352,000 for in January 1978. Jack had left the previous summer and John Neal, his successor, was a completely different manager, a far gentler and quieter man. We called him 'Jolly John' because he was always smiling.

He was appointed while we were in Australia on a post-season tour. We played a game in Adelaide and afterwards a club there offered me the chance to stay on and play six games for them on what was big money at the time – all my accommodation taken care of and I would also get 750 Australian dollars in my hand.

I stayed in a hotel called The Townhouse in the centre of Adelaide overlooking the cricket ground. After games, we used to go back to a restaurant and bar that one of the supporters owned and all the fans would be in there. If you scored a goal or played well, they would be putting money in your pocket. I'd never earned money like it in my life. I was coming away with pockets full of it from home games. It was a great experience.

Jack's departure had perhaps caused a little dip in my discipline, too. We stopped at Hong Kong en route to Melbourne on the way out and I met a young lady and somehow missed the plane. I had to travel down the next day on my own.

Luckily, I'd been at a bar with the British Airways crew because when I turned up at the airport with this ticket for the previous day and couldn't get on the plane, the captain that I had been drinking with the night before was there. I asked for his help and somehow he got me on the plane from Hong Kong down to Melbourne. Then I got in a taxi at Melbourne airport and had to knock up the late Willie Maddren to pay the fare for me.

I knew that Liverpool wanted me because Phil Boersma, who became a great friend and trusted colleague in my management career, had moved from Liverpool to Middlesbrough. Phil's big pal was a guy called Bob Rockcliffe, who owned the Wheatsheaf Garage in Knotty Ash that Bob Paisley used to go into every morning.

Bob Rockcliffe had phoned Phil to say, 'Liverpool want to buy your mate.' But Middlesbrough were reluctant sellers, they didn't want me to leave. Although I wanted to go to Liverpool, they kept saying they wouldn't sell me.

Then, suddenly, I got a call to go to the Queens Hotel in Leeds. They told me they had agreed a fee for someone to buy me, but I didn't know who because at the time Manchester City were also interested, and Leeds were, too.

I'd made my mind up, because of my situation with Phoebe and how good my life was in Middlesbrough, that if it wasn't Liverpool, then I would stay. Of course, when I walked in, I saw Bob Paisley sitting there, with Peter Robinson, the chief executive, and John Smith, the chairman. They were in a large ballroom for some reason, sitting at a big table when I arrived.

The minute I knew it was Liverpool, I was always going to sign and the deal took five minutes to agree. I then drove Peter Robinson back to Liverpool in the black BMW 3 Series I had at the time. There was a hump just as you come to the end of the M62 going into Liverpool and I was going too fast as we reached it. The wheels briefly left the ground and Peter let out a little scream.

My career was about to take off, too.

FIVE LEAGUE TITLES

When I arrived at Anfield in January 1978, I was joining the reigning European champions and a club that every northern European footballer aspired to play for. It was a special place, with an aura about it following two Uefa Cups, in 1973 and 1976, then the European Cup with a 3–1 win over Borussia Moenchengladbach in May 1977.

For me, even if I'd had been offered the chance to join Barcelona, Bayern Munich or Real Madrid, I would still have signed for Liverpool.

The secret of Liverpool's success lay inside the famous boot room at Anfield and the collective wisdom of Bob Paisley, Joe Fagan, Ronnie Moran, Roy Evans and Tom Saunders. These five wise men subtly created an atmosphere with their astute signings and clever psychology that ensured they had a dressing room full of players prepared to take the lead on the pitch and off it. That was their real genius.

Joe and Ronnie, in particular, would regularly say to us, 'Work it out for yourself, son,' and then walk away shaking their heads, as if to say they couldn't believe how stupid we were. That created a culture of responsibility, which is a quality that any title-winning team needs but is increasingly rare these days. So few modern players are natural leaders and it is often their managers who pay the price for that failing.

I knew from the outset that I would be coming into a ruthless dressing room with a winning mentality. There would be nobody to hold your hand. The higher up you go in football, the more that's the case. It was certainly true of Liverpool.

For years after I stopped playing, former adversaries would tell me that when they lined up in the tunnel against us, they felt we were a team of men. During my time at Anfield, the nucleus of the team was always a healthy group of late-twenties, and that intimidated opponents to an extent. We won some games, especially at Anfield, before they had kicked off because of that fear factor.

There were some big characters and egos in that dressing room. Emlyn Hughes and Tommy Smith spring immediately to mind when I first arrived at Anfield. Emlyn and Tommy didn't get on with each other, but all that was put to one side when a game was there to be won. That was the only thing that mattered on a Saturday afternoon in England or a midweek night in Europe. Winning.

As well as being the club to sign for, Liverpool were the scalp to take. Some teams would do a lap of honour if they got a draw at Anfield against us. Before kick-off, it was always drummed into us by Bob, Joe and Ronnie that it was the biggest game of the season for our opponents and we had to be prepared to match them in that respect. If we did that, our ability would take care of the rest.

I was 24 when I joined and not someone who would be intimidated, even walking into the most successful dressing room in European football at the time. I was determined to show that I deserved to be in their company and wouldn't let anyone down.

That's why my first title at the club in 1978–79 is one I remain particularly proud of. That team vies with the side I captained to the treble of European Cup, league and League Cup in 1983–84, my final season, as the best I played in. I find it hard to separate them when asked to, partly because one team gradually morphed into the other over my six and a half years at Anfield.

We had some incredible statistics in the league in that 1978–79 season. We amassed 68 points, a record under two points for a win, and lost only four games. Ray Clemence kept 28 clean sheets from 42 games and of the 16 goals we conceded, only four were scored against us at Anfield.

Can you imagine turning up to buy your season ticket and the guy at the window telling you that you would only see four opposition goals that season? How ridiculous does that sound?

I'd liken us to Antonio Conte's Chelsea now for younger readers.

We weren't always on the front foot, but we almost always got the job done. We had some special players that made the difference, but most importantly teams just couldn't break us down, as our defensive record at Anfield suggested.

In that season, my first full one, we started with 10 wins from our first 11 matches. We scored seven against Spurs at Anfield, including a Terry McDermott finish after a passing move from our own box to theirs which was named goal of the season. Later on, we lost only once from Boxing Day to the end of the season. We used only 15 players to win the title. Ray Clemence, Phil Neal, Ray Kennedy and Kenny Dalglish played in every league game and I only missed one.

If you look at the teams that have won the league of late like Leicester, the Manchester United teams under Fergie, Chelsea under Mourinho and now Conte, they didn't change their line-ups too much either. The modern-day emphasis is always on rotation, that we play so many games now and the game is a lot more demanding physically, but I don't really buy that. A settled team produces an understanding that can take you a long way.

We won the league again in 1979–80, if not as emphatically as we had the previous season. We started with a goalless draw at home to Bolton and were 16th after three matches. Our form remained patchy until Christmas, when we started to get going again.

Manchester United pursued us, but, just when it looked like they might overtake us they lost by six goals at Ipswich in March, on the same day we beat Everton at Goodison. We clinched the title at the start of May when we beat Aston Villa, while United lost at Leeds.

I only scored one league goal that season but my teammates came up with another 80. David Johnson got 21 of them, yet that didn't stop the club paying £300,000 for a thin, introverted Welsh lad called Ian Rush. Few of us could see why they had done so at first.

We then hit an 18-month slump when people started to write us off and say our era was over. We finished fifth in 1980–81 behind champions Aston Villa and Ipswich, Arsenal and West Bromwich Albion. We used 23 players that season, which was a lot by our standards, and our post-Christmas push failed to materialise as we lost six and drew five of our 17 league games from January onwards.

That malaise persisted into the following season and we were 10th at Christmas in 1981–82, when Bob Paisley offered me the captaincy. He'd had a couple of run-ins with Phil Thompson, my predecessor in the role. Phil had argued with him during a team meeting and that was that.

I'd tweaked my ankle at the time, so I was leaning against the goalpost during a training session while the rest of the players were doing some shooting. I was shouting, 'Wide, over the bar', generally taking the mickey out of their efforts. To my left, Bob shuffled up. He was always a man of few words.

'Would you like to be captain?'

'I'd love to be,' I replied, 'but, as I see it, there are a couple of people in front of me. Kenny's been here longer, and Nealy . . .'

'No, I want you to be the captain.'

I stressed again that I didn't want to cause any aggravation, but he just said, 'Leave that to me.' It was an example of the decisiveness and toughness that made him such a successful manager.

My first game as captain was an FA Cup tie at Swansea and we won 4–0, then went on a ridiculous run for the remainder of the season, losing only two more league games, away to Swansea and at home to Brighton.

When we clinched the title, Bob said it was his proudest one because we had made up so much ground, although he had to deal with a transfer request from his new captain along the way. This happened when I was out injured, having hurt my back playing golf at the same time that Bob was recovering from a bout of pleurisy.

I declared myself fit before a win over Nottingham Forest, but Joe and Ronnie, who were in temporary charge, said they would hold me back for a visit to Tottenham the following Monday night. The lads were all asking me if I was playing on the way down to London and I replied, 'Yes', having been told I would be, but then Joe came to the room I was sharing with Kenny Dalglish. Kenny was in the bath, and as an experienced player I sensed what Joe was going to say. Sure enough, he told me they had decided to go with the same team that had beaten Forest on the Saturday.

I told Joe he could 'stick his team up his arse' and then went down to the bar of the Holiday Inn at Swiss Cottage, had three gin and tonics and handwrote a transfer request. 'Due to circumstances, I feel it necessary to request a transfer, please treat this as a formal request and deal with it as soon as possible,' it read.

Bob then arrived at the hotel with a friend of his called Ray Pearce. He saw me in the bar and asked me what was going on. I handed him my transfer request in an envelope and said, 'You'd better ask them', as Joe and Ronnie were still in the restaurant with the other players having their pre-match meal.

Bob said, 'We'll see about that', and went off to speak to them. When he came back he told me I was playing, but I pointed out that I'd just had three gin and tonics. 'You can be sub then,' he said. I came on at half-time when we were 2–0 down and we drew 2–2, with Kenny scoring both our goals.

● ● ●

Bob announced he would be stepping down at the end of the 1982–83 season and we gave him another title as a parting gift. Some sentimental people suggested that we'd want to give him the FA Cup, the only trophy that eluded him and us in those great years, but that was nonsense.

Of course, we wanted to win it and would watch the final every year enviously, usually as we were either preparing somewhere for a European Cup final or on an end-of-season tour, but it never came above winning the league as a priority.

In my first two seasons, we came close, twice losing semi-final replays. Manchester United beat us 1–0 at Goodison in 1978–79 after a 2–2 draw at Maine Road, and in 1979–80 we drew twice with Arsenal at the same stage before losing the third replay to a Brian Talbot goal at Coventry. I nearly went for my teammates when I stepped onto the bus afterwards to find them singing, until Roy Evans explained he had instigated it to get us going again for the league. I calmed down after that and reflected that Pat Jennings' outstanding performances had been the main reason for our exit.

It remains a mystery that we could win four consecutive League Cups, from 1981 to 1984, yet fail when facing much the same teams in the more prestigious of the two domestic knockout trophies. We beat West Ham after a replay in the 1981 League Cup final, although I missed it with a bad back; then Tottenham in 1982, with Ronnie Whelan scoring twice, after extra-time. The 1983 final against Manchester United also went to extra-time, with Ronnie scoring the winner after Alan Kennedy had equalised a goal by Norman Whiteside.

Yet it was always the league that mattered most and we delivered it by April of Bob's final season as manager, with only a minor wobble in October, when we lost successive matches to Ipswich and West Ham. We beat Everton 5–0 in one of our finest performances, with Ian Rush scoring four of the goals.

We did slacken off after winning the title though, failing to win any of our last seven games. Bob tried to shake us out of it, but when he pulled the curtains closed in one team meeting, they crashed down on his head. We took the piss, literally so when we went for a glass of wine before an evening game and were still drinking at 5pm, but despite that we managed a draw.

I felt complacency was creeping into the club in this period and we needed a wake-up call. It perhaps came when we lost by four goals at Coventry in the December of Joe Fagan's first season in charge after a 15-game unbeaten run, but I was still determined to rouse us. I had words with Joe when we failed to finish off Manchester United, our main challengers, in the New Year and allowed them to escape from Anfield with a draw. I shouted that we had gone soft and told Joe, Ronnie and Roy that United would win the league and we would get nothing.

I was wrong in my prediction, not for the last time, but perhaps right in raising the issue at a key moment in the season. It was important never to let our standards slip and, as United faltered in the run-in after losing Bryan Robson to injury, we went on to a remarkable treble of league, European Cup and League Cup in 1983–84.

I scored the only goal in our League Cup final replay victory against Everton, but there was a scare in the second leg of our semi-final against Walsall at Fellows Park when a wall collapsed after we scored. It could have been a tragedy, like those the club would later suffer from, but was fortunately averted as the terrace was only a few steps high and fans were able to spill out onto the pitch.

I shouted to those at the back to ease the pressure further forward and also received a lot of publicity for a picture showing me carrying a small boy to safety. All I did was take him off someone else, who had lifted him out of the rubble and was staggering under the weight.

That 1983–84 team rivals the 1978–79 side as the strongest I played in at Liverpool. Overall, there were arguably more special players in the 1984 team, but in most positions it was nip and tuck.

For example, Ray Clemence was a top goalkeeper, but if you watch the 1984 European Cup final against Roma again, Bruce Grobbelaar is faultless in it; the amount of times he came out and took hold of the ball when we were under a bit of pressure. They were different, but equally good goalkeepers. Bruce had more courage, he was more prepared to put himself out there and make a mistake, and if he made one it was like brushing off dandruff or swatting a fly for him.

Terry McDermott could score 20 goals from centre midfield, Ray Kennedy would get into double figures from left midfield, Emlyn was England captain. Phil Neal and Alan Hansen were in both teams. Kenny and Dave Johnson up front became Kenny and Rushie, which was better, but there's still not a lot in it collectively. When Ronnie Whelan came into the team, he didn't get as many goals as Terry or Ray did, but he was a clever footballer.

If you pushed me to pick a composite team from those two sides, it would be a mixture of them. I'd go for Clemence; Neal, Lawrenson, Hansen, Hughes; Case, McDermott, Whelan, Kennedy; Dalglish and Rush.

What both those successful sides shared was a hard-working, compact midfield that was difficult to play through. There were no natural wingers – Craig Johnston would have been the nearest to a winger, but nobody worked harder. That was drilled into him. They spent time on him, coaching him and teaching him the position. Sammy Lee, Jimmy Case and Ronnie Whelan all got it without too much bother.

We still had some fabulous footballers who could be the difference in tight games, but, when the game wasn't going for us, we were almost impossible to break down. If you look at the 1983–84 season, we won many games by the odd goal, maybe not playing the best football, but with Rushie popping up with the winner.

Liverpool could play it both ways. On a Saturday, we could have a ding-dong on a muddy pitch with a lenient ref against an English team, and then go away to Bayern Munich or another big European team and turn them over in a game of football in midweek. We had that ability to switch from one to the other.

You have to remember what the pitches were like in those days, often resembling mud baths or worse. We were always told before a game, 'Match them for effort and you'll beat them, because you are better players.' In the first 15 to 20 minutes, our sole intention was to make the pitch big and keep turning the opposition back four. Then, once they stopped pushing up onto our midfield, we'd earned the right to start playing our football.

I knew Phil Neal, Alan Hansen, Phil Thompson, Mark Lawrenson, Alan Kennedy and Emlyn Hughes wouldn't give me the ball in that first 10 or 15 minutes. I'd show for it to try and pull an opposition midfielder in behind me. Then they would spin it in behind my marker and I would turn and support our strikers until we could impose ourselves on the game.

Was all this stuff coached into us? Yes, in the sense that we were encouraged to think for ourselves and solve problems on the pitch without needing to be told how to. Nothing illustrates that better than the time before my first Liverpool game, at West Bromwich Albion.

It had been the usual week of training: a jog round the perimeter with Ronnie Moran, a few stretches and some 80–90 per cent sprints, finishing with a five-a-side. Five days of that. In the dressing room at the Hawthorns, at a quarter to three, I am looking round and the senior lads are all there – John Toshack, Steve Heighway, Ian Callaghan – but nobody has revealed what the plan for the game is yet.

Joe Fagan was the mildest man. In my seven years with Joe, I bet I heard him raise his voice maybe half a dozen times, but he exploded when I asked what was expected of me.

'I've been here a week and no-one has spoken to me,' I said. 'How do you want me to play?'

It was a naive inquiry, as I soon discovered from Joe's eruption. To hear him, you normally had to lean into him because he spoke so quietly, but this time he replied in a big booming voice.

'Eff off! We've spent all this money on you and you're asking me how to play football?'

With that, he turned and walked away. Can you imagine a manager saying that to any player today?

I come back to that saying that you would have heard every day in training and at half-time in every match: 'Work it out for yourself, son.' They treated you like men, not children.

They certainly knew the game. Could they express themselves? Joe could, Ronnie would quickly lose his head with you in frustration at times and the boss would put it in a way which very few people understood – but they all understood the game inside out.

I quickly got the Liverpool way. Kenny quickly got the Liverpool way. We understood we were part of something that was there before us and would still be there long after we'd gone. You knew you had a duty to behave in a certain way at the football club and that came from the senior professionals. It was passed down from each team to the next as the success kept coming.

It must have gone back to Bill Shankly's time, to old values, players like Ron Yeats, Ian St John and that mob, with the fearsome Reuben Bennett as Shankly's enforcer on the coaching staff then. They gave them direction, but also responsibility.

In the modern game, there's zero responsibility. Our big characters were encouraged to remain big characters. It didn't make them immune from criticism. When I walked into that dressing room, the players were all powerful. You quickly worked out who were the big personalities and the lesser lights. You must have good senior profes-sionals, but no-one wants to take responsibility anymore.

It wasn't Bob always telling you that you had to behave in a certain way. It wasn't Joe, Ronnie or Roy either. They guided you in football terms, but they let you be a man and said, 'The senior players will guide you, learn from them.'

We had some fabulous players who bought into the team ethic and always put that first and were willing to be responsible if things weren't going well. Other teams wanted to knock us down, but it was all credit to the players that if it wasn't the biggest game for us, we always appreciated it was the biggest game for them.

The manager had very little to do and say, because with any issues that came along the senior players dealt with them. As I slowly became a senior player and then captain, I like to think I did that.

The three strongest voices in the dressing room, the biggest in terms of decision-making, were me, Kenny Dalglish and Alan Hansen. We quickly established ourselves as the next generation of leaders coming along.

When I went back to Liverpool as manager, after seven years away – two in Italy at Sampdoria and five in Glasgow at Rangers – I remember asking Ian Rush and Ronnie Whelan what had happened to the dressing room.

'The kids don't listen anymore,' they replied.

'Kick them in training then,' I said. 'I'm not going to say anything.'

Responsibility is about putting yourself out there to be criticised. Making decisions on the pitch and being a big voice in the dressing room and telling people they can do more, despite knowing that flak could always come your way. Emlyn Hughes, Phil Neal and Tommy

Smith did that when I first arrived. Ray Clemence had a bit to say, too, while Steve Heighway was the voice of reason.

After a game, if we hadn't done well, the papers were full of 'Souness didn't do his job, Dalglish missed a sitter and Hansen was sloppy at the back.' When do you read that today? It's all about the manager – his tactics, his substitutions. Do you ever see players get any stick? They avoid any criticism.

Until we get back to something like that, our game will not prosper. Enjoy it while it lasts, but if we keep going down this road where the players are constantly allowed to get off the hook, it will end in tears. A manager can't go in and nail anyone anymore. It's more like, 'See in the second half, could you maybe try a wee bit harder.' That's how ridiculous it has become.

That's why I saw what was coming for Jose Mourinho when he subbed John Terry at Manchester City in the second game of the 2015–16 season. I was working for Sky and right away I said, 'He's just caused himself one almighty problem there.' Terry came out and said all the right things, but I bet he would have thought, 'Oh, really?'

If Bob Paisley had done that to me, as captain of Liverpool – in order to make a point to the directors that he wanted more players, as Mourinho did – my relationship with him would have finished there and then. I believe that was a major reason for the subsequent demise of Mourinho at Chelsea.

You can't fall out with players today, because if you fall out with one he has two or three really close pals and very quickly you could end up with half the dressing room against you – and half the dressing room might be worth £200 million.

Fergie was perhaps the last manager who could win that internal battle. He made Roy Keane his bulldog in the dressing room, but then Keane challenged Carlos Queiroz, his assistant, and ultimately had words with Fergie. If Roy felt he was on an equal footing with Fergie, he soon discovered that wasn't the case.

We were more grown up and didn't earn as much as today's players do. At 31, and as captain of Liverpool and Scotland, if I'd tried to offer an opinion at a team meeting, Joe and Ronnie would have been standing over me ready to clip me round the ear, more or less saying, 'What have you done in the game to warrant having an opinion?'

In my last management job at Newcastle, in contrast, I was standing in front of people with 20 or 30 games under their belts offering up opinions. Players who had never won anything, and never will, were telling me how to do it. Is that because there's a culture of opinion nowadays? Players today seem to get away scot-free.

The Germans are more prepared to take that responsibility as players, and that's a fundamental reason why they do consistently well in international competitions. There's a culture of taking responsibility in their national team, whereas too many of our players today turn up, train, have their shower, their lunch and then get out of there as soon as possible.

At Newcastle, three of my senior players gave a collective sigh when I asked them to stop speaking to a critical local journalist. 'I am not sure we can do that, we live here,' they replied. It was a watershed moment, when I knew I had no chance at Newcastle because of players not willing to take responsibility and say, 'We are all in this together; win or lose together.' Instead, it was a real every man for himself moment, and I knew then I was not going to be successful there.

Although I perhaps didn't realise it at the time, the senior players in the 1984 Liverpool team – Kenny Dalglish, Alan Hansen, Phil Neal, Mark Lawrenson and myself – cajoled the others to the treble. All five of us were not scared to point out to others what needed to be done.

I like to think that when the younger lads might just have been getting into their armchairs, we got after them. That would show in training when you would go around and have a kick at a few of them. Looking back, those five senior players hounded and chased anyone who was slacking.

Kenny and I would fall out on a regular basis. Then we would be sitting next to each other on the bus on the way home and rooming with each other. We looked after each other on the pitch, too. I was ruthless at times, but 90 per cent of that was me getting back at an opponent who had done something outrageous to me or one of my teammates. That was allowed in those days, and accepted as just the way it was.

You also saw players unceremoniously removed from the team at times. That happened to many of those around me between 1978 and 1984; guys like Emlyn Hughes and Phil Thompson, who were key members of the side. So you knew nobody was untouchable.

In the days when there were only two subs allowed, I'd be sitting getting changed after an international week, along with two team-mates, both of whom had played internationals for their countries in midweek, and maybe another five, six or seven guys not getting changed, who had all also played for their countries.

I would often think to myself: I am captain, I've won things here, but if I have a bad game today, they are going to wonder why I have had a bad game. If I have another next week, they are talking among themselves, saying, 'Better keep an eye on him.' In the third game, they would be thinking that I should be left out of the team.

You were only ever a couple of games from them having a close look at you. Joe would sit you down and ask, 'Everything alright, son?' It never happened to me, but I know that's what he used to say to players before they were dropped.

The dressing room was a self-managing dressing room. We'd play Saturday, be off Sunday, then come back in on Monday. If we weren't playing until Wednesday, or it was a week off, Joe and Ronnie would say, 'Free day today, pick four teams and go and have a round-robin competition over there.'

They would then walk to the other side of Melwood, an area which was called Wembley, and it would be the injured players and the staff playing the kids. The staff team always won. That went back to Shankly, too. They would still be playing at one o'clock until they won. They always had to win.

Maybe you wanted to stroll around in these games because you'd had a big night on the Sunday, but it never happened because there were people there who would always make them competitive. Maybe Terry Mac and Big Alan Hansen would sometimes fall into the strolling category. Emlyn Hughes loved his social life too, but he wanted to win every single five-a-side, so although he was feeling rough he would be bang at it.

Other than those two rascals, Hansen and McDermott, those games were always ultimately fierce. They would start off friendly and then somebody would start chipping away, someone else would try and empty another in a challenge and it would all become very competitive very quickly and the staff knew that. They knew the men they had.

Of the title winners since, Fergie's United were the closest to us in maintaining success over a period of time. In many ways, they were a better watch when they were flying, but we were better at keeping the ball than they were, which served us so well in Europe. They always had at least one winger in Ryan Giggs, while we never really did, but we were harder to play through than they were.

I don't think it's a coincidence that United also had a really successful period when they had players who felt responsible for each other because they were all local boys and this was their club. As I said, when I went to Liverpool, I quickly got what playing for Liverpool meant. You can compare that to United's group. That was their cycle and when the last ones left – Paul Scholes, Ryan Giggs, Fergie himself – the standards slipped. It's hard to reproduce that togetherness once it's gone.

A question that's frequently asked of me is: 'Could you have played in the modern game?' My first reaction is to laugh. The protection from the referees and the standard of the pitches are the two obvious things that jump out as positives. Liverpool were a passing team when I played for them. We weren't a team that went from back to front, pushing in behind or nicking things from set pieces. We were a proper football team. So, on both those counts, it would have been easier. The referees would have allowed us to play a lot more and the pitches would have, too.

The question I would throw back is: 'Could the players today have played in our era?' I just love it when someone nowadays goes to cross a ball or have a shot, but they blast it over the bar. Or a pass doesn't go where it should and they look down and shake their head and stamp as though they are putting an imaginary divot back on a perfect pitch. 'It wasn't my fault, there has to be a reason for it,' they seem to be saying.

All our training was about one- and two-touch, so we could move the ball quickly. You can't play any quicker than that, so it makes me chuckle when people say we would struggle with the pace of today's game. Okay, you can't pass back to the goalkeeper now, he can't pick it up, but that's the only change. We would still take the sting out of games, because we could keep the ball among the outfield players in any case.

I firmly believe the modern game would have suited us down to the ground and we would still have won the league, maybe more times than we did. The best team wins the league. That's why I remain so proud that we won it five times during my six full seasons at Liverpool.

THREE
EUROPEAN CUPS
4

I remember when I was manager at Newcastle United, Craig Bellamy and Kieron Dyer were dismissive of my era as a player and all the trophies we won at Liverpool during that time.

'When you played, it was walking football,' they claimed.

'Tell me this then, because I have never been able to work this one out,' I replied. 'We didn't live very well. We lived quite recklessly at times, in fact. We drank too much beer and had too many late nights, but all those teams we played, the Italians, the Germans, they were all doing what you do now, yet when it came to the last half hour or extra-time, we used to finish a lot stronger than them. Can you explain that to me?'

Part of the answer is that Liverpool played possession football so well that we made the opposition run about more than we did, but we could also dig deeper than them when required. We were playing against teams on zero alcohol, proper diets and they simply couldn't live with us in the later stages of games, either physically or mentally.

I remember the ball going out late on when we were playing the 1984 European Cup final in Rome and Roma's goalkeeper, Franco Tancredi, screamed at the ball boy for getting it back to him too quickly. They just wanted to get to extra-time or penalties, despite being in their own stadium in front of their own fans. We had such inner belief that we thought we would win it, one way or the other.

In those days at Liverpool, you were never allowed to believe you were the finished article. They always left a bit on you, Joe Fagan, Ronnie Moran or Roy Evans, that made you feel you still had a bit to do to win their respect. They would say, 'We've had really good players here, you're a good team, but not like the players we had in the past.' You were always made to feel that you weren't quite as good as the group before and it spurred you on to each league title and each European Cup. Those trophies were evidence that you were as good as or better than your predecessors.

Our European rivals did not know quite what to make of us at times. I remember one pre-season in Marbella when we turned up at our hotel and the reception was full of bikini-clad women and billboards advertising that Liverpool were coming to town.

The typical British club manager would have been thinking of his players in that environment, 'Oh no, we'll not be able to control them', but in the tournament we did well against Bayer Leverkusen, Malaga and Real Betis despite the distractions.

We were sunbathing down by the pool by day and having a few beers by night. Leverkusen's coach, Dettmar Cramer, who had led Bayern Munich to the European Cup twice, would be sitting watching us. He'd have one beer all night and we were doing what British footballers did at that time, which was to have a few more than that.

He'd get his players up at six for breakfast, train before it became too hot, then get them back into bed, lunch, then train again at night when it was cool. We'd get up late, train in the midday sun when we should have been lying low and then the next night we were out again. But when we played them we battered them.

He was in the bar after the game looking at us and had the courage to come over.

'How do you do it? You are drinking beer all night and you can play football like that.'

Our response? 'We're maybe having a bit more than your players, but our senior pros will say enough is enough when we've got a big game.'

We weren't saints and enough could have meant three, four or five pints of lager, but we understood when to call a halt. We were given licence by the club. They knew we would go out and have a few beers, but they also knew that at the right time we would shut it down and behave ourselves.

Cramer became more puzzled still when he saw us play for the second time in four days, against one of the Spanish sides, and we were fabulous again. Everything he thought he knew about football and how to look after his players had just gone right out the window.

I often thought the club arranged the pre-seasons to be as difficult as possible for the players, almost hoping we would get beat up, which we never did, so they could have a right go at us to do more before the season started. Looking back, that was probably the psychology on their part.

Nobody was allowed to think they were something special, as I quickly discovered on my first European trip with the club in 1978. Having signed in January, I wasn't eligible to play against Benfica in the European Cup quarter-final that season but I travelled to Lisbon with the lads, who came from a goal down to win the first leg 2–1.

It was pouring with rain and after the game everyone was covered in mud, apart from me. I was standing there with my latest gear on thinking, 'I look pretty sharp', when Ronnie Moran came up to me.

'Is there something wrong with you? You're not part of the team, so start picking the stuff up.'

There was me with my best clothes on picking up these muddy, sweaty strips. I had been the most expensive signing between two English clubs at that point and that was them saying, 'Who do you think you are?' I did the chores because that was the way it was at Liverpool. We didn't have a kit man, everybody mucked in to load the skips with the dirty strips, tying the socks together and so on. Ronnie, Roy and Joe were in charge of that, so if you were told to help, you helped.

After beating Benfica 4–1 at Anfield, Liverpool faced the side they had beaten in the previous season's final, this time in the semis. Borussia Moenchengladbach wanted revenge and I came on as substitute as they won the first leg 2–1 in Germany.

The second leg was the first time my parents had watched me play for Liverpool. I helped to create our first goal for Kenny Dalglish before Jimmy Case and Ray Kennedy added further goals to put us through with something to spare. The final would be at Wembley against FC Bruges of Belgium.

I got a lot of credit for putting a perfectly weighted pass in for Kenny to score the only goal of that final. The reality was that as it came out of the sky to me on the edge of the Bruges box, I was aware that people were coming to close me down, so I felt I would just go in strong and win it. Fortunately for me, the dink fell nicely for Kenny and he did the hard bit.

Mum and Dad came to the final, as did Phoebe Haig, my landlady at Middlesbrough. They were staying in the Holiday Inn at Marble Arch and I left the after-party at Swiss Cottage and went over to show them my medal. Mary Stavin, the former Miss World, was my partner for the night, but it was my parents I wanted to share the moment with more than anyone else.

Here I am at 25, having just won the European Cup, with a former Miss World on my arm and I have the big shiny gold medal. It doesn't get any better.

At about three or four in the morning, I went over to the hotel and got my parents out of bed. I knew they were extremely proud. My dad would have loved to be a professional footballer. I was living his dream, so that was very special.

● ● ●

Although we won three European Cups in the seven years I was at Anfield, I still feel we should have won at least one more during that period. Nottingham Forest did a number on us in the 1978–79 tournament and deservedly so, as I learnt a harsh lesson about staying in my position.

We had started that season superbly in the league, including that 7–0 win over Tottenham, and I got carried away when we were 1–0 down with three minutes to go at the City Ground in the first leg of the European tie. I went chasing the game from central midfield and ended up in the Forest left-back area.

The ball was played in to where I should have been, then back out to the left wing, from where it was squared and they scored to make it 2–0. Joe tore a strip off me afterwards. We would have taken 1–0, definitely, but 2–0 made it doubly difficult for us in the second leg. Forest got a goalless draw back at Anfield and we were out. That was a lesson about staying in position which I never forgot for the remainder of my Liverpool career.

What Brian Clough achieved with Forest, winning the European Cup in 1979 and 1980, was arguably the greatest feat of any English manager, considering that group of players and that size of club. They didn't play a particularly attractive brand of football, but we had problems for a few years beating them. We would have most of the ball against them, but still end up on the losing side. They had a hoodoo over us.

Their strength was their defence and midfield: they had no-nonsense Larry Lloyd and Kenny Burns at the back, and were workmanlike in the centre of the park with the likes of Ian Bowyer and John McGovern. They also had a great goalkeeper in Peter Shilton. They defended on the edge of their box at times, but they had my old Scottish schoolboys' pal, John Robertson, the most underrated player of my generation, on the left wing as an attacking inspiration, along with Trevor Francis, who would later become a good friend when we played together at Sampdoria.

There was no shame in going out of Europe again in the first round the following season to Dinamo Tbilisi, the best team I played against in European football in that era. They had six or seven of the Soviet Union team and they got an away goal at Anfield in the first leg through Aleksandr Chivadze to leave us trying to protect a precarious 2–1 advantage.

The second leg was an arduous affair. We had to travel to Tbilisi via Moscow by Aeroflot, the Soviet airline, and were kept in a tiny room at the airport while they searched every piece of our luggage and conducted a painfully slow immigration procedure. Our hotel in Georgia was poor and so was the food. I survived on crisps, chocolate and shortbread while we were there.

On the eve of the match, we were treated to their fans marching round our hotel with torches chanting *'Dinamo! Dinamo!'*, which did not help either. They even had a police escort for it.

During the game, the ball boys couldn't get it back into play quickly enough while Tbilisi were behind in the tie, but, as soon as they had the lead, they strolled to get the ball and sometimes even kicked it away from us.

It was all unnecessary, as Tbilisi were good enough to beat us without all of the gamesmanship they used or the promise of upgraded apartments from the Soviet regime if they got through. They won the second leg 3–0, with Chivadze scoring again, from the penalty spot.

Years later, I was at the semi-final of the 2006 World Cup in Germany, Italy against Germany, and was walking to my room at the hotel when someone came over to me and I thought, 'I know him from somewhere.' It was Chivadze, who clearly had fonder memories of our encounter than I did.

At least we survived the first round the following season. After a 1–1 draw in Finland in the first leg, we beat Oulun Palloseura 10–1 at Anfield. I scored a rare hat-trick and so did Terry McDermott.

We liked to have a bet each season of around £100 on who would score the most goals. Terry always made sure he mentioned this in front of the other players, so I couldn't back down. Then, around Christmas time, he would say, 'Well, are you ready to pay me yet?' Sure enough, I had to hand it over every Christmas, with me on two or three and Terry on about 15 goals by then.

Next, we faced a Battle of Britain against an Aberdeen side managed by a certain Alex Ferguson. Bob Paisley was an old fox and made a point of talking up Gordon Strachan beforehand, saying he was worth £2 million. In his early days, Gordon needed a ball for himself at times, he spent so long on it, and Bob was encouraging him to keep doing that.

Aberdeen fancied their chances, but we were far more experienced in Europe than them. Terry Mac chipped Jim Leighton to score a wonderful goal as we won 1–0 at Pittodrie and there were a few tasty tackles in the game. We flew back from the Lossiemouth RAF base that night, our plane surrounded by all these military jets stationed on the runway.

When they came to our place we won 4–0, and I think it was a wake-up call for that Aberdeen team that they still had a bit to go to compete at the highest level. I'm sure Fergie must have learnt from it, because they would win the Cup Winners' Cup in 1983.

I scored my second hat-trick of the tournament against CSKA Sofia in the quarter-final, and I have to say it was a cracking one, with the second and third goals coming from shots outside their box in front of the Kop. It meant that I shared the top-scorer honour in that season's tournament with Terry Mac and Karl-Heinz Rummenigge.

He played for Bayern Munich, our semi-final opponents. I missed the home leg through injury and it finished goalless. So we went out there and the Germans thought they were firm favourites. They had leaflets on every seat showing the quickest route to Paris for the final. Bob came in and said, 'Eh, have a look at that', and pinned one up on our dressing room door.

It was the one and only time in my seven years at Liverpool that we did anything special tactically. We had already been out to warm up, then the buzzer went for us to go out for the game and Bob suddenly said, 'One thing tonight, Sammy [Lee], you mark Paul Breitner.'

We were all going 'What?' We hadn't practised it, we had no clue. Whether Bob had woken up that morning and thought it might be a good idea to put someone on Breitner, or whether he had been thinking of it since the first leg, I don't know, but it worked a treat. Sammy kept the boastful Breitner, who had forecast they would beat us easily, quiet on the pitch.

Kenny went off early on with a twisted ankle, but Bob brought Howard Gayle off the bench and he tortured them with his pace until they started kicking him. Bob then substituted the substitute when Howie, who would never back down from a confrontation, began to retaliate.

Ray Kennedy got the goal with six minutes to go and you know then that's you safely through to the final. Although Rummenigge equalised in the 88th minute, we went through on the away goal. Afterwards, I couldn't resist putting my head round Bayern's dressing room door and saying, 'See you in Paris', before heading back to our celebrations.

The final against Real Madrid was a real meaty game. There was some heavy duty stuff going in early on, and the pitch was poor. I remember the ball coming back to Phil Thompson, who was standing maybe two yards inside our box. The lines were limed onto the pitch about two inches proud and the ball kicked up around his waist. Despite the magnitude of the match, we all laughed, but it could have been a penalty.

I tried to leave a bit on Jose Antonio Camacho, the Spanish international defender, and from the side Uli Stielike, the German midfielder, came in and caught me. Fair play, you live by it and all that, but it was right on the outside of my calf and it was stiffening up. Just before Alan Kennedy scored the goal to win it, I was going to come off. I remember at half-time in the dressing room, I was just walking round because I knew my calf would turn to concrete if I didn't keep moving it.

After the game, Phil Neal and I got hauled in for the drugs test. By the time we managed to pee, we came out to an empty stadium. We found a bus outside with British journalists, thinking they would be going back to the centre of Paris, but they worked out where we were going and where they were going was no good to us, so halfway round the stadium we got off the bus. It was now pitch black and nobody had come to say we'd get a taxi or there would be a car for us. We were off to celebrate and we were on our own. Can you imagine that today?

They had put a half-kilometre perimeter round the stadium, there was a real police presence and they would not let anyone near it unless they had a ticket. We walked for half an hour and no taxi would stop.

'The first blue light that comes along, I'm out in front of it,' I said to Phil.

Sure enough, a police van appeared, blue light flashing, and I was straight out in the road waving it down. The back doors opened and three or four guys came out with big sticks and I was like, 'Whoa, whoa', showing them my medal and pointing back to the stadium.

'I've been playing football in there.'

They seemed to accept my explanation, because they threw us in the back of the van and took us to our hotel. Talk about how precious the players are today. Did I ever mention that to Bob Paisley and Joe Fagan? I didn't dare, although I might have said, 'Thanks for waiting for us', to the players when we got back.

● ● ●

Then came those missed chances to win another European Cup, ones that still gnaw away at me now. If Forest and Tbilisi had been worthy winners against us, I felt we let ourselves down by not going further in the tournament in the 1981–82 and 1982–83 seasons.

After overcoming Oulun Palloseura comfortably again, we came through two tight games against AZ 67 Alkmaar of Holland 5–4 on aggregate to reach the quarter-finals. We would face CSKA Sofia, the same side we had beaten 5–1 at Anfield and 6–1 on aggregate at the same stage of the previous season's tournament, but they had improved and we also suffered from some shocking decisions in the second leg. We went to Bulgaria with only a 1–0 lead this time, courtesy of Ronnie Whelan's goal, but thought Ian Rush had provided the precious away goal until the Austrian referee incredibly waved play on after their goalkeeper pulled the ball back from behind the goal line.

Stoicho Mladenov then scored when Bruce came for a cross he had no chance of getting to, and Mark Lawrenson was sent off. So we faced extra-time with 10 men, having already lost Terry Mac to their violent tackling. Although we hit the woodwork three times, Mladenov added a second in extra-time and we were out.

The following season was a similar story. After coming through comfortably against Dundalk and HJK Helsinki, we got beaten in the quarter-finals by Widzew Lodz, a Polish team we should never have lost to. Bruce was at fault for their two goals in Poland, and I was at fault in the home leg after Phil Neal had put us ahead with a penalty.

I was in the left-back area and opened my body out, kicking towards the Anfield Road end, to give it to Nealy, but he hadn't gone, so I hesitated. Then he went and I played it, but someone read the pass and Bruce brought him down for a penalty from which they scored.

It finished 3–2 and I blamed myself for our exit. I don't think it was a particular problem we had with Eastern European teams, although the travel there was always troublesome in those days. My recollection is we were beaten by two very ordinary sides.

There had been a three-year gap from my first European Cup with Liverpool to my second, and it was the same cycle before my third in 1984. After a comfortable 6–0 aggregate win over Odense of Denmark, we showed we had matured from the previous two seasons by coming through a tough tie against Athletic Bilbao of Spain. They gave a polished performance in leaving Anfield with a 0–0 draw from the first leg, one we would have been proud of ourselves.

That's what we were famous for, for being a tough nut to crack. The second leg in Bilbao was a big game for Liverpool, and a coming of age for us as a team on the way to winning the trophy that season. It comes back to responsibility, to helping your mates when things aren't going well. Ian Rush scored the only goal with a downward header, but we all performed well and I was proud of my own perform-ance that night.

Bilbao had a reputation as a rough team. Andoni Goikoetxea, their centre-back, was known as the 'Beast of Bilbao' after a horrific tackle that put Diego Maradona out for three months, but they were good losers against us, especially their fans, who clapped us onto our bus and also passed round their leather drinking pouches.

They were a good side, who went on to win the double in Spain that year. Better than Benfica, who we overcame in the quarter-finals. Ian Rush again provided the only goal at Anfield. Portugal wasn't as pleasant as Spain had been in the previous round, as they pelted us with oranges and coins when we went out to get a feel for the atmosphere. Bruce threw one back at them, but our real riposte was a 4–1 win at the Stadium of Light. I almost missed that match, after my mother's death back in Edinburgh beforehand left me in a state of shock, with flu-like symptoms of feeling hot and cold, but I felt better on the morning of the match and played in the evening.

The intimidation you encountered in Europe in those days always brought the best out of me for some reason. I actually enjoyed it and that helped me survive our semi-final ties with Dinamo Bucharest. In the first game, Lica Movila was man-marking me and I got frustrated because the game wasn't going particularly well for us. He pulled my shirt as I was trying to run into the box and I swung round and hit him and broke his jaw in two places. It sounds terrible now, but that's the way the game was then. He'd tried to leave a bit on me, so I retaliated.

We won 1–0 through a Sammy Lee header. As it was the Eastern Bloc back then, the players always had their secret police watching them. They jumped out at you with their leather coats and were all huge. People reading this now might not understand, but there was a chance of the players defecting at any time. They would get to the West to play the game and try to stay there if they could.

As I was coming off and approaching the top of the stairs at Anfield, I don't remember any of their players having a go at me, but then I saw Movila with the broken jaw and a towel packed with ice tied in a bow around it. I started laughing at him, but behind him were these two big secret police guys and they started getting all aggressive with me until Ronnie Moran, who was a big powerful man himself, jumped in and told them where to go.

So we went to Bucharest and got off the plane and onto the bus. I was sitting there minding my own business when there was a knock on the window. I tried to ignore it, but eventually I looked round and the guy's head is level with me and I thought, 'How big are you?' He was a giant. He was making an eye-gouging gesture at me, certainly not a goodwill one, so I said, 'Not me, him', and pointed to where Alan Kennedy, who also had a moustache and curly hair, was sitting.

The Dinamo players made some threats of their own as the game started. Their captain, who had played up front in the first leg, had moved back into midfield for the second leg to play directly against me. He gave me a sinister, knowing smile and a thumbs-up, but I just smiled back and focused on staying out of the way of their wild tackles, and making my passes. I put Rushie in for a goal after 11 minutes with one of them and although they equalised and the fouls became increasingly fierce, Ian scored a second with 15 minutes left to make sure we would go through.

It was a big old-fashioned arena and to get to the dressing rooms you had to walk across a running track and up a hill. I said to big Bob Bolder, our reserve goalie, 'Just stand behind me as we're walking off here.' We got away with it. We got into the dressing room and Joe stood in the middle and went, 'Right, shut up', and when it all went quiet, he screamed, 'You effing beauty!' at the top of his voice.

We hoped we were going to play Dundee United in the final, but then the news came through that they had been cuffed by Roma, which meant we would face the Italians instead – in their own stadium. More intimidation seemed certain.

Yet we were relaxed. We went to Israel for a week's holiday, came back and trained at Anfield and Melwood and practised some penalties. Stevie Nicol scored and the rest of us missed.

The Israel excursion was, I suppose you would say, a bonding trip, not that we needed it. On it, there were a couple of Italian journalists who had been sent to try and get interviews and see what we were up to. As captain, I said, 'Why don't you come and join us for a drink, an aperitif before we go out?'

It lasted for four or five pints before we went out to a good Chinese restaurant with a big long table, where we could all sit together. The two Italian journalists were there having a Campari and soda or whatever, while the boys were having four or five bottles of Maccabi beer. They were looking at us, thinking, 'No chance.'

They would still be sitting up, to the very early hours, to see us come back in. We'd all be rocking and rolling and singing, having fun, when we did return. They just thought, 'This team hasn't a prayer', because the Roma team had gone to a secluded hotel to prepare and were playing in their own stadium, training there every night at the right time for kick-off, while we were having a jolly.

They wanted us to do a press conference in a room at the airport when we arrived in Rome, but Joe rejected that. We trained in the stadium and then Kenny and I, rooming together as usual, went to our beds. Kenny took a sleeping pill and within 10 minutes he was unconscious, but before he fell asleep he would talk away in a language I've yet to identify, far less understand.

There was constant noise from the room next door. Eventually, I phoned down to reception and they said, 'Yes, I'll see to it, sir', because the television was blaring. I tried banging on the walls. Nothing. I went outside and battered on the door, too. Nothing.

In the morning, we got up and were leaving the room and it was Joe Fagan coming out of the one next door.

'Boss, you kept us awake all last night,' I said.

'Sorry, boys, we opened a second bottle of Scotch last night and had to finish it.'

So the manager had kept his captain awake all night.

We couldn't train on the morning of the game because the pitch they had provided us with was a ploughed field, so we returned to the hotel for lunch. At the end of it, Joe stood up and tapped a spoon on his glass.

'Excuse me, boys, can you leave us now,' he said to the waiters.

They did so and it was as if Joe was talking to himself.

'Big team, big match, must be a good team,' he mumbled. 'Some good players, some of them have won the World Cup, but I tell you what, they can't be as good as us. Now the bus leaves at 5.30, make sure nobody is late.'

That was our team talk. It was the only time I can remember Joe referring to the team we were playing against, although he never mentioned any of their players by name or went into any detail.

We got to the stadium and it was quite full early on. I suggested we should go for a walk round it, to show we wouldn't be intimidated by the atmosphere. We walked all the way round and we even tried to walk past their hardcore fans in the Curva Sud until the police said, 'You better not go there, stuff is being thrown on', but we had taken the sting out of them anyway because we had shown the Roma supporters, in their own stadium, that we weren't frightened.

In the dressing room, Alan Hansen was telling stories and we were sitting there listening to him, still with our suits on. Joe had to say, 'Any chance you could get changed because we are playing in half an hour.' We went out, warmed up, came back in and we were in the tunnel and we had such a togetherness. It was ridiculously relaxed.

I think it was David Hodgson who started singing the Chris Rea song, 'I Don't Know What It Is, But I Love It'. Not just singing it but booming it out, and we all joined in. The Roma players looked at us in disbelief. Bruce was dancing around, while there was fear in their faces. It was a big game and we were treating it as a laugh.

We scored first through Phil Neal, in his fourth European Cup final, but they deserved their equaliser from Roberto Pruzzo and it went to extra-time then penalties. Cue more dancing from Bruce as we won the shootout 4–2. Steve Nicol, who had scored when we practised them, missed and the rest of us, who had missed, scored. The Roma fans behind the goal were shouting abuse at us and the Italian photographers were deliberately setting off their flashes as we stepped up, but I ignored all that as I slotted mine past Tancredi.

● ● ●

Liverpool had won their fourth European Cup in eight years, an incredible sequence of success, and a real indictment on the performance of the England national team of that era. They failed to qualify for the 1974 and 1978 World Cups and struggled to the 1982 finals in Spain. They also failed to make the 1984 European Championships in France, the same year we beat Roma in Rome to win the European Cup.

The argument was that it was too much of change of style from the old First Division to elite football in Europe, but at Liverpool we pooh-poohed that idea with our performances and a squad full of British and Irish players. We were the counter-argument to that lame excuse. We could go and take on the best in Europe in a game of football midweek and come back and meet the challenge on a Saturday afternoon at a muddy Baseball Ground, Derby County's old stadium, with its quagmire of a pitch.

That was the beauty of our team then, but we weren't alone as Forest (twice) and Aston Villa also won the European Cup in that period. Seven years out of eight between 1977 and 1984, an English club, packed with British players, won the tournament. All the talk of 'our league doesn't help us when we go to play European football or help the national team'. Yet we all did it.

We could throw that switch between the two. Our league has not always been the most technically sophisticated, but there's always been an honesty attached to it, and that's because supporters demand the game is played a certain way, but the trick was to play a different style in Europe and we could.

English clubs have struggled to repeat that sustained success since. It was 15 years before one won the European Cup again, and Manchester United looked beaten by Bayern Munich in 1999 until they scored two goals in stoppage-time through Teddy Sheringham and Ole Gunnar Solskjaer. Liverpool's incredible win on penalties over Milan in 2005 was another case of coming back from the dead, as they won it from 3–0 down.

When United beat Chelsea on penalties in the 2008 final, it was probably as strong as English football has been in Europe since our time. Chelsea nicked the final on penalties in 2012 but, as they had been against United in 1999, Bayern Munich had been much the better team for most of that match.

There has been a one-off feel to each of these triumphs, of a team at full stretch to win the tournament and needing some luck to do so. Nobody since has been able to repeat or sustain their success in Europe as we did.

In the early 1980s, all the best players in the world went to Italy, but how many European Cups did their sides win compared to England's in that era? Juventus did, in the tragic circumstances at Heysel in 1985, but none before that.

Serie A then was like the Premier League today, a world league, but they couldn't win the European Cup because you need a team, not just individuals. Paying the best money and having the biggest players doesn't necessarily mean you will win it. In theory, they should have been dominating the European Cup, but they didn't.

I certainly don't see the Champions League as more difficult to win now. You get a chance, because it's not a knockout, to have one bad night and remain in it. Are you going to have six bad nights? It gives you a chance to get your feet under the table and get a bit of momentum going domestically as well. Then, when you get into the knockout stages, it's also the second half of the domestic league when you should be bang at it for fitness and being up to speed.

The whole Champions League concept was designed by the big European clubs who wanted guaranteed income, six games, with three of them at home. Yet it has become a procession, it's the same teams every year, give or take one or two that get into the knockout stages.

What the big clubs wanted, the big clubs have. Yet it's ironic that both Milan teams, who would have been party to that decision-making, are no longer regularly involved. Now, more changes are coming because they want back in. Again, they are driven by money and are likely to exclude big clubs in smaller countries such as Rangers and Celtic in Scotland or Ajax in Holland. Uefa need to do something to stop that process or their flagship tournament will lose more of its appeal.

When I played, you had to win either the First Division or the

European Cup to qualify. It's now the top four in the Premier League and again that's all about guaranteeing more money for the big guys. That's how Arsene Wenger has kept his job at Arsenal, by finishing in the top four for the last 20 years until last season. If only the league winners qualified, would he still be at Arsenal now?

That's deemed success because it brings in X-amount of revenue. The difference between the leagues is greater now than it has ever been because of that money. The German league, the big guys in Spain, the Premier League, although we have not really made our mark, and Paris Saint-Germain in France see most of it.

I'd like to see it back as a straight knockout tournament. I find in the Champions League group stages some games mean nothing. The last and second-last games can be dead rubbers in the current format. You can get into a position where you can rest players and you see some soulless matches. I remember going to watch Feyenoord play at Juventus in Turin in 2002. It was in the 69,000-seater Stadio delle Alpi, but there were around 10,000 people inside it for a group-stage match.

Look at the numbers. They don't get big crowds for every Champions League group-stage match throughout Europe. We kid ourselves on that. We look at Barcelona, Real Madrid and Bayern Munich and what happens in our country, but beyond that the gates go down significantly and teams often don't play in full stadiums.

When I played, Spanish football was extremely cynical, while the Italian league was dull and all about counter-attacking football. That only changed when Arrigo Sacchi's Milan came along and won the

European Cup in 1989 and 1990, with a style that was very similar to Liverpool's.

They were well-organised and difficult to play against, but also had some very special players like Franco Baresi, Ruud Gullit, Frank Rijkaard and Marco van Basten. They played 4–4–2 with a tight midfield and didn't try and go and win the game in the first 10 to 15 minutes.

They were about the closest in style to us of the great European sides since and the outstanding side of that period. It wasn't Johan Cruyff's Barcelona, who had a solitary success in the tournament in 1992 against Sampdoria at Wembley through Ronald Koeman's free-kick, but were then crushed 4–0 by Milan, then managed by Fabio Capello, in the final two years later.

You know what, I don't buy all this talk of the modern Barcelona playing the 'Cruyff Way'. They didn't win the European Cup again until 2006 under Rijkaard and their triumphs since, against Manchester United in 2009 and 2011, and Juventus in 2014, were all achieved with an outstanding generation of players led by Leo Messi and the wonderful Andres Iniesta.

Everybody has tried to follow the Barcelona way of playing, but that really is a mistake because the players that Barcelona have are of such high quality. Even their full-backs are like ball-playing, tricky midfielders who can deliver the killer pass when they reach the final third. When you have lesser teams trying to play like that, they look vulnerable because they are giving the ball away in dangerous areas.

Barcelona were so good five years ago, arguably the best club side we've seen, they could win playing that way – but I don't think they can do that now and I can't remember anybody else playing that way and winning. The Milan teams didn't. The modern Real Madrid teams, who have won it for the last two seasons, are not always on the front foot, there is also a pragmatism attached to their football.

We are always looking to emulate other countries. France won the World Cup in 1998 and the Euros in 2000, so suddenly we should be doing what they are doing. Spain are the next super nation, winning the 2008 European Championship, the 2010 World Cup and then the 2012 European Championship, but it's one generation of outstanding players, not a procession, that they produce. It's a cycle. It was the French way, then it became the Spanish way. We have to look beyond that.

That doesn't mean to say you can't still have a St George's Park or more coaches and better facilities, but it was a cycle they found themselves in. Otherwise France would have produced another group after the Zinedine Zidane generation that won the World Cup and the European Championships. Closer to home, there would have been a new Class of '92 at Manchester United.

There's no holy grail. It's a large slick of luck. Even if you have a good set-up and coaches that know what they are doing, they are in the hands of the gods. They are not going to produce a new Zidane or a new Messi just like that. For sure, if such a player comes along, they can certainly help them on their way.

Left: December 1969. A fresh-faced trainee at Tottenham Hotspur.

Below: February 1976. Now with Middlesbrough, and competing with Leeds United's Frank Gray at Elland Road.

Above: Signing for Liverpool, alongside John Smith, Peter Robinson and Bob Paisley, in a function room at the Queens Hotel in Leeds in January 1978. When I turned up, I didn't know which club was signing me until I walked into the room.

Left: Celebrating a Kenny Dalglish goal in the European Cup semi-final versus Borussia Moenchengladbach at Anfield in April 1978.

Right: The following month, with Kenny Dalglish again and Ray Kennedy, this time with the European Cup. We'd beaten FC Bruges 1-0 at Wembley.

Left: Scoring against Manchester City at Maine Road in August 1978. I'd slightly miscontrolled the ball, but was then able to fire it in with my left foot.

Above: We called it 'The Jock Picture'. With Kenny Dalglish and Alan Hansen after winning the Charity Shield against Arsenal in August 1979.

Right: May 1980. In the bath with a bottle of bubbles, Terry McDermott and the First Division trophy.

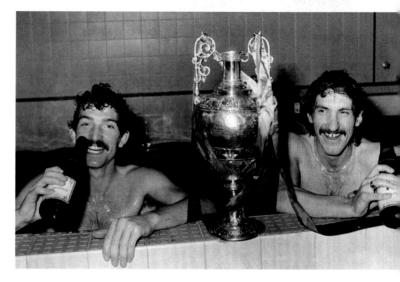

Above: Another 'Jock Picture'. May 1981. With Messrs Dalglish and Hansen again, this time with the European Cup. We'd beaten Real Madrid 1-0 in Paris. It was a very physical encounter.

Left: With Bob Paisley before extra time in the 1983 Milk Cup final against Manchester United. I was very lucky to have been managed by Bob, and was very close to him.

Below: It had to be a good strike to get past Neville Southall. Celebrating my goal against Everton in the 1984 Milk Cup final replay.

Above left: I had a wonderful relationship with Joe Fagan. We're about to receive the 1983-84 First Division trophy at Anfield.

Above right: Scoring my penalty in the shoot-out against Roma in Rome in the 1984 European Cup final. After I'd put the ball down to take the penalty, I uncharacteristically changed my mind and sent the ball to the keeper's left instead of to his right.

Left: The sheer joy of lifting the 1984 European Cup.

Right: It's June 1978 and I'm playing for Scotland against Holland in Mendoza at the World Cup finals in Argentina. We won the game 3-2 but could only finish third in our group.

Left: At the 1982 World Cup finals in Spain, competing against the USSR in Malaga. The game finished 2-2 and, again, we couldn't get out of the group. In those days the USSR included the likes of Ukraine, Georgia, Belarus, Latvia and Lithuania: they were a strong side.

Right: I had the great privilege of working with Bob Paisley, Joe Fagan and Jock Stein, but perhaps only Jock would have adapted sufficiently to have been successful in this modern era of football.

Right: Scoring a penalty versus England at Wembley in April 1986.

Left: One of my trademark whole-hearted tackles against the Danes in the 1986 World Cup finals in Mexico.

Below: The game against West Germany in Queretaro was played at 7,000 feet and in 100-degree heat. After the game, I suffered the worst exhaustion I'd ever experienced.

Left: With
Trevor Francis
at Sampdoria,
September 1984.

Below: Tackling
the great Diego
Maradona,
a fabulous
footballer.

If English clubs are to reassert themselves in Europe, they need to stop trying to copy other countries and develop a style of their own. One that's different to what they do domestically, and based on defending and keeping the ball better than they do at the moment. That was the secret of Liverpool's success at home and abroad when I played, and it can be again for the British clubs.

GREAT TEAMMATES, GREAT PLAYERS

To give you an idea of how highly I rated my teammates at Liverpool as we won those three European Cups and five league titles in my time at Anfield, I'd argue that only two Liverpool players since that era would have got in those sides.

We would have found a place somewhere for Steven Gerrard and Luis Suarez, although I'm not quite sure where.

Steven Gerrard has been the best Liverpool player since then, but does he replace Terry McDermott in central midfield? I'm not so sure. Neither Gerard Houllier nor Rafa Benitez completely trusted Steven as a central midfielder, because he didn't naturally sense danger when Liverpool didn't have the ball and therefore wasn't filling spaces to stop it developing. So he would have had to play in the wider areas for us. He's not going to play instead of me, because he's a different kind of player, and I'm not sure he would have provided more for us than Terry Mac did.

Ideally, you would want both of them in the team, getting 20 goals each from midfield per season. That would have made life easier for all of us. We would have had to shuffle the pack a bit, but Steven gets in our team somewhere.

So does Luis Suarez, but where I have no idea. I wouldn't want to be the manager making the decision. Good luck breaking that one to Kenny Dalglish and Ian Rush.

Does that not tell you how good a team we must have had in those days? When you look through the last 30 years and think there's only two Liverpool players since who would have got in it?

Kenny was a false number nine. But that's a new thing, and it's nonsense. Neither Kenny nor Ian were old-fashioned English centre-forwards, like a Jeff Astle or a Geoff Hurst. If everyone knew where Kenny was going to play, he would be easily marked. If people knew where Rushie was going to be all the time, he would have been marked, too.

We played with the majority of the ball, but all those coaches that we played against, at home and abroad, could never work us out. They tried system after system: three at the back, one up front, men out wide, playing an extra midfielder. They could never work out why we would have the ball all the time, apart from the guys being very good players.

They said we were a classic 4–4–2 team, but that's wrong. We were more of a 3–5–1–1, if you want to put some numbers on it, with our full-backs pushed into midfield and me sitting behind them, but in front of the two central defenders. We were such a fluid team, constantly changing and reacting to each other, so our formation was always changing, too.

You had to be intelligent and good on the ball to play in those Liverpool teams. We perhaps weren't the silkiest side, but we all had the ability to take the ball and move it on in two or three touches at most. As I said earlier, all our training was one- and two-touch, the idea being it would improve your first touch. It had to be good because the second touch was going to be your pass, so the ball had to be in the right position to make that pass.

They say the game is quicker now. Well, how much quicker can you move the ball than one- or two-touch? The pitch would certainly make the game quicker today, but when the ball comes to you, how much quicker can you use it than one- and two-touch? That's all our training was. That was the so-called 'secret' of it.

The thing that decides how quickly the game is played is how quickly your brain deciphers the picture. When you see average players playing football, they receive the ball, take a couple of touches and then get their head up.

All the top men have a picture in their head every time a ball is passed from one player to another. They have a different picture each time, with each pass, because they are thinking, 'I might receive the ball here, what's the picture?'

The dummies watch the ball being passed among their teammates and then, when the ball comes to them, that's the first time they are thinking about a picture. You weren't a Liverpool player if you didn't have that picture in your head.

Nobody in our team had that gift more than Kenny. He wasn't the quickest, but he had that sixth sense that would tell him where everyone was all the time. He could read the game several steps ahead. His brain worked at a different level to the vast majority of players. He could anticipate things. He was also extremely courageous and had wonderful technique.

He was like a big cat, prowling round the jungle, looking for victims: the opponent that was asleep, who he knew he could turn inside out. He'd work out pretty quickly who was the opposition's weakest link. If there was someone he felt he could get pinned, with his back to goal, and roll them, he'd work out who that was. If someone was dreaming and not in the correct position, he would work out who that was. He was always looking for someone to prey on.

Ian Rush had that same anticipation as Kenny, plus electric pace. Rushie would turn his back on a goalkeeper who had the ball. He would give him the opportunity to throw it to a full-back and would pretend that he wasn't looking or interested and then, out of the corner of his eye, spot the instant the goalkeeper threw the ball, and would be sprinting in at the defender. Then we would all respond behind that. That was our pressing. They talk about pressing from the front now, as though it's a new thing that never happened before. Oh really?

My abiding memory of Rushie is of tap-ins that he made look very simple by being in the right place at the right time. He was never blasting it. He did strike shots with power occasionally, but mostly his goals were tap-ins. He made the person who had the ball play it to where he wanted it with his exceptional movement. He was making your mind up for you.

He was so rapid that if he got in a race with a player, he would generally win it. If the ball came into the box and had a bobble, he would be first onto it with that anticipation again. It's a recurring theme with great players: anticipation and having a picture in your head. That's what separates good players from great ones.

Both Kenny and Ian were as brave as lions, too. It's the hardest place to play football, up front, particularly playing with your back to where you want to go. You are turning blind, you are being asked to put your head on things when there's a lot of heads and elbows flying around in a six-yard box and the goalmouth.

I remember playing against Manchester United at Anfield and the ball was fired up from our back four or goalkeeper and Kenny came short to flick it on, and, as he flicked it on, Kevin Moran led with his elbow and Kenny turned into it and smashed his cheek. I was the first on the scene and by this time Kenny was up on one knee and had his hand over his face.

'Are you okay?'

'Yeah, I'm alright,' Kenny said. 'Give me a minute.'

I pulled his hand his away and immediately said, 'You're not okay.'

The whole of his cheek had caved in. I went to see him later that night in hospital and they had put a metre of gauze packing into his face. He was tough. You couldn't sicken Kenny, he would take anyone being physical with him as a personal thing. There was the Glasgow boy in him, and he was impossible to intimidate.

Kenny and I had several stand-up arguments. We had to be pulled apart at Coventry one day when we were losing 3–0.

'Any danger you can get hold of the ball up there and get us started?' I said to him.

'Any danger you can win it, so we can get started?' he replied back.

We were two of the biggest guys in the dressing room and Ronnie Moran and Joe Fagan would just stand back and let it happen. They were not going to interfere, because they knew everybody in the dressing room would sit up and take notice of two big players coming close to blows, far more than anything they could say. They loved that. There was no job for them to do.

Kenny and I were the most vocal. Alan Hansen would dip in and out of the meetings, with a more balanced outlook. We would get a bit too excited. Kenny was the shop steward. Nobody ever won an argument with Kenny, he always had to have the last word.

Alan would look at any issues from both sides; he was cute and clever. He had a sense of humour and good banter. He was somebody that nobody wanted to take on in an argument, because he could kill you with a one-liner. Depending on what was happening, the three of us would back each other up and were quite a formidable threesome in that dressing room.

Outside of Liverpool, Alan never got the credit he deserved for the type of player he was. He was greatly underrated. When you talk about a modern-day footballer, he ticks all the boxes. Was he good on the ball? He certainly was. Was he quick? He certainly was. Was his decision-making good? It certainly was. Could he head the ball? No, but he would make sure the guy he was marking didn't get a clear header on goal.

He was great for me because if I was getting picked up in midfield, he was confident enough on the ball to suck players in. I would take three steps to the side, the guy who's marking me would go to Alan, he'd slip a perfectly angled pass to me and I was free and we were away, moving with our passes, the picture developing and changing again.

When you see ordinary centre-halves receive the ball deep, the minute a striker makes a move towards them, even though he could still be six or seven yards away, they pass it square to the full-back or the other centre-back. That means the striker is still in the game.

Alan would suck them in instead, allow them to get two yards away and either angle a pass or skip past them, and then that striker is dead, out of the game. He had the confidence in his ability to do that. You couldn't get the ball off him in a telephone box, he had that much technique. He was a midfield player in disguise really.

Phil Thompson and Mark Lawrenson, Alan's partners at centre-back, both had a period in midfield when they were younger, too. Thommo had a fabulous career, given that physically he wasn't the strongest. He worked at his game and had a fantastic attitude to it.

If you are talking about a player who made the most of his God-given assets, the ones he was born with, Thommo comes into that category. He would always be there, sweeping up or intercepting, because he was reading the game. He wasn't tall or particularly good in the air, neither was he the quickest, but he never got exposed because he had such a good football brain.

Lawro was different. He was more athletic, aggressive and quick, the perfect foil for Alan. He didn't have the anticipation that Thommo or Alan did, but he liked to get physical and loved a tackle.

On a Saturday afternoon in January with a muddy pitch, Lawro would be covered in mud in the first 15 minutes because he wasn't reading it like Alan. Alan would come off after 90 minutes and his shorts and shirt would be clean like he had just stepped out of a sports shop window.

With Lawro, I always felt he could have got there earlier, but just liked to leave a bit on the opposition player. He could have read the play and anticipated it, but I'm convinced, although I've never asked him, that he would slow down occasionally just to let the striker know he was there.

I also played with Emlyn Hughes at the start of my Liverpool career. He was a great organiser, very vocal and loved a challenge. Emlyn was a natural captain, a real warrior type, who got involved in every aspect of the game. He could play a bit, too, as a marauding type of centre-half very different to Alan Hansen and Phil Thompson. They were cultured and anticipators, but Emlyn had very good athleticism and used that. He was a big influence on the team when I went there as a young man.

Generally, you were playing against two strikers in those days, so our system used to be the two centre-backs, with the goalkeeper, Bruce Grobbelaar or Ray Clemence, standing on the 18-yard line when we were up the field. The two centre-backs would mark two strikers and I would patrol, if you imagine a clock, from nine o'clock to three o'clock in front of them, depending on what side the ball was on. If the ball was on the right, I would shuffle that way and vice versa if it was on the left.

My main job was to try and stop them being exposed. If we were attacking and lost it and the ball was played upfield to the opposition strikers, I'd try and get myself back in that patrolling position. So they were going to have to play a high ball to get it into the striker, or one struck long over the top to get into a race with our centre-backs, because I would be able to cut off anything played in on the ground.

It was more physical in the 1970s and 80s, and before that, because you had to take an extra touch a lot of the time as the ball was bobbling up at you from different angles, and that would encourage a challenge. Whereas today you can play one- and two-touch on the modern pitches. What are the big changes in football? People are quicker, but have their brains become any quicker? I very much doubt that. The game has only become quicker in the sense that the pitches are better.

It also makes me smile when I hear people talking about how full-backs join in these days and are more like wingers than defenders, because I played in three European Cup finals and in two of them our full-backs, Alan Kennedy against Real Madrid in 1981 and Phil Neal against Roma in 1984, scored from open play.

What people never really worked out was that our full-backs used to play in midfield. They were quite happy there. When I got the ball, the two full-backs were further forward than I was, and that, in turn, pushed our wider midfield men further forward and the opposition back towards their own goal.

You look at players today and if they win an FA Cup, or if they win one league title, they have had a great career. Just have a look at what my Liverpool teammates won. How would you describe their careers?

Nobody has more medals than Phil Neal. Eight First Division Championships, four European Cups and four League Cups. What a career he had. He never really gets mentioned as a great, but he should be because he was one.

Every day in training, Ronnie Moran would be up front during the warm-up and Phil had to be on Ronnie's shoulder. He had to be the leader of the group, every single day. Every day was cup final day in training with Phil. You need good senior players. He was a 10 out of 10 in that respect, someone who turned up for work every single day.

With Alan Kennedy, it always seemed he felt lucky to be at Liverpool, whereas the majority of us felt they were lucky to have us. That might sound terribly arrogant and big-headed, but if you are a big player, you feel you are one. You don't say it, certainly not at Liverpool then, but you think it. There were six or seven us who felt that way, whereas Alan was one of the few that thought, 'I'm lucky to be here.'

Belly Boy was well-liked in the group, one of the really popular guys in the dressing room. He would have a go physically and in our system, because he had great energy and athleticism, he was a good player. Bob Paisley said one day when he was having a poor game that they shot the wrong Kennedy, but Alan would never let you down, he always wanted the ball regardless of how he was playing.

If the ball came into the box, he was going to put his head on it, even if it meant getting himself hurt. He never shirked a challenge. In training one day we were in a circle, keeping possession, two in the middle and Alan was one of them. Terry Mac whispered to me, 'Trip him up when he comes over,' and I said, 'You trip him up.' Anyway, I tripped him up and Alan's chinned me. I've gone for him and they get hold of us both, but he gets loose again and chins me a second time. He was forever up for a challenge.

With a different personality, Stevie Nicol would have been talked about as a true great, too. He was happy to drift along, Bumper. I can never remember him getting upset and being nasty to anyone. He was happy just to be one of the chaps. Easy-going, likeable, amiable are all words you would use to describe him. In terms of quality though, he was definitely a Liverpool great.

If you asked me now, 30-odd years later, I still don't know what his best position was. Was it left-back, right-back or centre-back? Was it central midfield or right or left midfield? He could play anywhere in the back four and anywhere in midfield and it would be all at the same quality. If you had injuries during a game, he could go and play wherever you wanted him to.

People might argue for John Barnes making it into our midfield, but he didn't do it for me when I went back as manager. Besides, the great Liverpool teams I played in never really had wingers, with the exception of Steve Heighway. They would come in narrow when we didn't have the ball and give us width when we did have it, but they weren't the kind who wanted to have a go, one-on-one with people. They would get half a yard and whip the ball in, but they weren't the jinky types who wanted to run at defenders and dribble past them.

I reckon I could have played with anyone beside me. In the position I played, my job was to move the ball as quickly as possible, to get it forward to the people that mattered. Bryan Robson and I would have been a great partnership, but I don't wish I had played with anyone else because I was blessed with the guys I did play with.

The partnership I had with Terry Mac was a special one. How many goals would Bryan Robson or Steven Gerrard have got in our team? Would they have got any more than Terry Mac? I don't think so.

From current players, Terry was similar to Tottenham's Dele Alli with his ability to get goals from midfield.

He's mainly remembered as a goalscorer, but he was a fabulous all-round footballer, too. With Terry, you think of his great engine up and down the pitch, but he was also full of technique and had a really good football brain. You are doing him an injustice if you just talk about his athleticism.

It's like people saying about me, 'Oh, that Souness was tough.' I like to think that's secondary to the other qualities I had. You don't win what I've won if you are just a thug.

The best player in a team is not necessarily the silkiest or most eye-catching; he's the most influential. How do you compare a centre-forward with a goalkeeper? The best player might mean someone who goes to war for the team and is prepared to stand up to any kind of challenge that's thrown his way, not the guy who's getting the tap-ins, scoring 25 goals a season and running to the crowd with his arm up.

Ray Kennedy was another great teammate and player, another with great football intelligence. He was a striker to start with at Arsenal and won the double with the Gunners, alongside John Radford up front. As a young man he honed those striker's instincts. Then he came to Liverpool and ended up as a wide-left player, who, when he saw the game developing on the other side of the pitch, timed his runs to the far post to get tap-ins or headed goals there. Ray was also clever enough to fill the position defensively. He was a top player.

Jimmy Case was the same. He had a brain and could see the way a game would develop. He was a lovely striker of the ball, always chipped in with goals and knew how to fulfil the defensive side of his role as well. That four in midfield, Jimmy, Ray and Terry and me, was the strongest unit I played in.

Jimmy really should have been at Liverpool longer, because he went on to play well into his mid-thirties at a high standard. I think they became fed up with his lifestyle – he liked a night out or two, let's put it that way. The end came when he got pulled over for drink driving.

Both Ray and Jimmy would stand their corner against anybody. We had a formidable and physical midfield and would have been difficult to play against. Gradually another midfield evolved, as people were phased out around me. Sammy Lee replaced Jimmy on the right. He was also a lovely striker of the ball and knew the position and what was expected from him, having been at Liverpool as a schoolboy. Even older players, brought in from elsewhere, would have learnt from Sammy's attitude to the club. He lived in the city centre of Liverpool and understood it better than anybody. I think we all learnt from him. We'd feed off his passion for the football club and the city, but he was a good footballer, too.

Ronnie Whelan is another player who was underrated. He got into the team as a left-sided midfielder, replaced Ray Kennedy and then gradually gravitated to a more central role beside me. He was a very good footballer who developed a nasty streak as his career went on.

Ronnie could leave his foot in and there were very few who would want to be tangling with him. He wasn't overtly aggressive, but at the same time Ronnie was no shrinking violet. He was an elegant, quietly-spoken Irishman, but on the other side of the coin, not someone you would want to mess with.

He didn't have a powerful physique, but he was great at intercepting just about everything because he could read the body shape of the guys he was playing against and see where they would be trying to pass it. He was always in the right place at the right time, and that was no coincidence.

Ray Clemence, our goalkeeper, used to stand on his 18-yard line, but they say that's another new thing of course, holding a high line. Well, we used to push up the park and hold a high line. We knew we would be caught out occasionally; eventually, someone will break the line, someone will break the offside trap. We never set out to play offside, but we would if someone was running forward without a brain. If they went early, we would just stand and hold our line.

That meant we were compact as a team going up the field and coming back down it. The staff felt the benefits of doing that over nine months, in a season of 60 games, would far outweigh the times when we might get caught holding that line. In modern times, Barcelona work on the same premise. It might be risky but long term it pays off.

Clem was a wonderful keeper. He and Peter Shilton played alternate games for England. Clem was better coming off his line, Shilts arguably better on it.

Clem fancied himself as a player and would join in the five-a-sides, just as Bruce Grobbelaar, who succeeded him, would. You couldn't go near either of them. They would play there on a Friday afternoon and their elbows and their knees were liable to injure you on the day before a game. Both thought they could play. In reality, they couldn't. I've never had the courage to tell them that, but they were both top goalkeepers.

People poke fun at Bruce, but he was wonderfully athletic. He just played in the wrong position for his personality. Really, he should have been a centre-forward, running away to the Kop after scoring yet another goal. He wanted to steal the show, but had all the qualities you would need of a goalkeeper. He was brave mentally and physically.

He would come out and make a mistake, drop one, and you would concede a goal from it, and the next time an identical ball comes in, he's out for it again. If you ever need an example of going into the lion's den and being a team player, it was the 1984 European Cup final in Rome. Bruce came out of his goal time and time again against Roma. He claimed cross after cross that night. It was a perfect display of goalkeeping, but he couldn't resist the drama of the penalty shootout. It's remembered for his showmanship, the jelly-leg wobbles as the Roma players came up to take their penalties, as much as us winning, but he was faultless that night.

It would be really hard to pick between them. Clem perhaps, because he was more reliable, yet Bruce would put his neck on the line more than Clem in terms of, 'Don't worry, guys, I am going to take the pressure right off you here.' His policy was, 'I will come for everything.' Over a career of 15 years, there's going to be so many advantages to that. I know people might speak about his mistakes, but they should also remember the good things.

● ● ●

When you are making comparisons between generations, what you have to say is that great players from the past would still have been great players today. Then when you talk about the very elite it becomes about opinions.

I didn't see Alfredo Di Stefano, but they say he was a great. The best player in British terms, Bob Paisley, Joe Fagan and Bill Shankly would argue, was Tom Finney from Preston. They would have had him in any of our teams at Liverpool.

We would also have found room at Liverpool for Lionel Messi. Even at my best, I wouldn't have got near him. Messi has the most advanced radar of any player I've seen; he's aware of incoming threats and works out well in advance how to evade them. He's a problem solver, a game changer, the greatest player to have played the game. I don't say that lightly, but I've been saying it for a while now. I don't believe that I've seen, or that I'm likely to see, anyone better in my lifetime.

What younger football supporters have to understand is that players such as Messi and Cristiano Ronaldo don't come along in every generation. We are in a golden period, watching two of the best players to have played football.

If we go back to the period before Messi and Cristiano Ronaldo, who were the greats? Zinedine Zidane was a great, so was Thierry Henry, the other Ronaldo, Ronaldinho, but all those players are still short of these two. They were not at this level.

I can't remember any player from history consistently influencing games as Messi has. The world's best when I was growing up was Pele and he would have been a great player now, too, but Messi surpasses him. He's also way out ahead of Diego Maradona – it's not even a close call anymore.

They say that Messi has not won the World Cup and that Maradona single-handedly won Argentina the 1986 tournament. I disagree. In the Champions League, Messi is playing against the same defenders he would face in a World Cup and he makes them look like novices.

I often argue with Hugh McIlvanney, my *Sunday Times* colleague, over this. It can get quite lively at times between us when we get onto the subject. I feel Maradona allowed himself to get out of shape midway through his career. Having played against him several times, there's no doubt he's up there in that group of the best four or five players to have kicked a ball, but greatness comes not just with doing wonderful things, but with longevity. You have to factor that in.

Messi has been doing it for well over a decade now, that's why he is streets ahead of Maradona and anyone else out there. I was in the Nou Camp when he scored four against Arsenal in 2010. I've watched him single-handedly win games for Barcelona over and over again. He's sensational.

Let's not forget that Maradona failed to leave an impression at Barcelona after moving there from Boca Juniors in 1982. People say that he dragged Napoli and Argentina to their titles, which suggests the other 10 players were bang average, but there were lots of good players in both those teams. Careca at Napoli and Jorge Valdano with Argentina spring immediately to mind. We have this imprint on our minds of the goal he scored against England when he ran from the halfway line, but Messi goes on runs like that regularly.

I know the game is less physical now, but I assure you that every time he goes out onto the pitch the defenders and aggressive midfielders playing against him are trying to leave a bit on Messi if they can. Nine times out of 10 he will come up with the correct answer to what's in front of him. Whether that's somebody trying to flatten him, doubling up on him or pushing him in a direction he doesn't want to go in. You can't stop him. All the coaches and football brains have tried. We are dealing with a special footballer here. You can put all the bear traps out there and he will just skip over them.

I have stood next to him on the pitch at the Nou Camp when we were doing the match build-up on the touchline with Sky and he's tiny, but he just has the most unique technique and football brain. He has the athleticism, the speed, the change of direction, but he's also such an intelligent player. When goalkeepers and defenders think they've got him, he manages to get shots away when nobody expects him to. He's got a sixth sense that very few footballers have, past or present.

When I managed Galatasaray, they also had a professional basketball team. Two Americans joined it and used the gym at the training ground. I talked to them about Michael Jordan and said, 'In our game, we would test him physically.' They simultaneously shook their heads and said, 'No, no, no, the coaches would say, just leave Michael alone, he's going to get his 30 points or whatever. If you upset him, he's going to get 50.'

Messi's the same. If you set out to kick him, you provoke him. We saw that when Barcelona won 3–2 at Real Madrid in April 2017 and he scored the winner after being caught by Marcelo's elbow earlier in the game.

Cristiano Ronaldo is unlucky that Messi happens to be around at the same time. He's in the top five to have played the game, too, but Messi is better. He's more giving than Ronaldo, more appreciative of teammates.

You see that in a simple thing such as their goal celebrations. Ronaldo does his matador stance, whereas Messi runs to his colleagues for a cuddle. It's far easier to like Messi's on-field manner than the arrogance Ronaldo shows, but it could be the other way round because I don't know either of them personally.

There's not a lot between them, though. What puts them above all the other players you could mention, is that they do it so consistently. Nearly every week, they both score ridiculous goals. The main difference is that Ronaldo, because of his physique, is better in the air, but then I can remember Messi scoring with an excellent header in the 2009 European Cup final against Manchester United in Rome, when Barcelona won 2–0.

That's the only obvious advantage, but Messi is a better dribbler than Ronaldo. You can go on forever talking about where each of them has the edge over the other, but it boils down to who is the biggest influence on their team, and that's Messi for me. He is more of a team player than Ronaldo.

If you look beyond them, who is the next Ronaldo or Messi? You can say that Suarez is a fabulous player, or Gareth Bale or Neymar, but they don't come anywhere near these two. None of them will reach the heights or records of Messi and Ronaldo. Not a chance.

So enjoy them while you can, because they won't be around forever. Kids today are blessed to be part of the generation that has grown up watching them, just as I was blessed to play with so many great players and teammates in my time at Liverpool.

THREE WORLD CUPS

Scotland have not made it to a major international tournament since the 1998 World Cup, while England have always fallen at the quarter-finals, or earlier, since hosting Euro '96.

I played in three of the five World Cups for which Scotland qualified consecutively, between 1974 and 1990. In my own career, I always argued that we should have recognised that as an achievement in its own right for a nation of just five million people. I got criticism for saying so, but time has proven that I was right.

Going beyond the group phase of the finals always eluded us; we were nearly-men at that level. We always had three or four top players, but you are only as strong as the weakest point in your team and we also had players, without naming names, who were never up to it. Could we have done better? Yes, for sure. You can look back at individual games and think we shouldn't have got beaten there. Overall though, we were always just short of a team that could have gone a long way in a World Cup. We certainly had players in each World Cup who were up to the standard to do that, but not the whole team.

The same has been true of England when they have hit their own, higher, glass ceiling at major tournaments. They are a quarter-final team at best and in the last two tournaments, World Cup 2014 and Euro 2016, they haven't managed to reach that stage, finishing bottom of their group in Brazil and losing ignominiously to Iceland in France.

If we had three or four players who could get in most teams in my time, England had five or six. Have they ever had seven, eight or nine? No, they haven't and they have a population the best part of 60 million to choose from. It's a numbers game. They have never had the seven, eight or nine top men you need to win a World Cup. This has been going on for generations, for decades, so it's more than just bad luck. Scotland don't qualify because we are not good enough anymore. England don't get to the semis or the final because they are not good enough, ultimately.

That has led to disenchantment with international football, to an extent, on both sides of the border. If we were doing well, those conversations wouldn't take place. People talk about there not being a great interest in international football, and that's because the nations aren't performing.

Qualifying for European Championships and World Cups would be deemed a success for Scotland, although that wasn't the case in my playing days. For England, it's a different marker. They think they should be getting to semis and finals on a regular basis and maybe winning a major tournament. The two nations are falling out of love with international football because it ends in disappointment. They feel their players could and should do better.

It's not because international football has suddenly become secondary to the Champions League and Premier League. If we had been more successful, it would still retain its interest for us. We saw that at Euro 2016 when Wales, Northern Ireland and the Republic did well in France. Look at how those nations responded.

There is always a feeling that when the British teams go abroad, we don't do very well, because we are in what they call in Italy *ritiro*, literally in retreat, where we are locked up in a hotel or in training camps. We find that difficult.

There was a bit of that in my generation. Players found they were going stir crazy, because it wasn't something they were used to, but the modern player accepts that far more readily. It helps when they have private charter planes that fly them between the very best accommodation available, where they can relax between games. So there are no excuses there.

England have gone to the opposite extremes in recent years. In South Africa in 2010 under Fabio Capello, they isolated themselves in Rustenburg in an Italian-style *ritiro*. In Brazil, under Roy Hodgson, they embraced the tournament more, staying and training in Rio. Neither paid off. Maybe there's still an element of British players simply struggling with a long period away from home; or maybe, as I have already explained, they are just not good enough.

The profile of professional footballers has never been higher, so they often want a bit of peace and quiet but not total isolation. My own view is that players are best not locked away, that there should be a bit of interaction with the locals, and that people should be allowed to come and go in the team hotel to a certain extent.

The downside of putting players in a situation where they can integrate with the public is that it's not beyond certain newspapers and magazines to throw a few girls into the mix and see if they can get a story out of it. The only way forward for these players is relative isolation, because there will be so many people trying to cause them problems, whether it's those who have had too much drink around the place or certain parts of the media looking to make mischief.

I know it didn't work in South Africa, but that's because England weren't very good, not because of where they stayed. Ideally, you would want to be out of the city, with a golf course to break up the boredom for the players. It is about keeping them entertained without them going mad. For Fabio Capello, an Italian, Rustenburg would have seemed an obvious base for an international team.

Is it a coincidence that Italy often do well at World Cups and there's never any issues with being away for a long time? The Germans built their own secluded training camp in Brazil, but they are also just better professionals than we are, ready to accept they are going to spend a month away from their families if they get all the way to the final. There's no feeling of being in prison, no feeling of must get out and have a beer. They are there to do a job.

The dynamics of a squad are no different to any other walk of life. They are not all going to love each other but they are a team, they have to go there and get on with each other. Little cliques will develop, and as a manager you have to look out for that, but the overriding factor is they are there aiming for the same thing, which is to be as successful as they possibly can on the football pitch.

What you have to do as a manager is take away every single excuse when it comes to the facilities. I am thinking of Saipan and Roy Keane's exit from the Republic of Ireland squad in 2002, because of the team's ramshackle preparation for the tournament and what he saw as the substandard training facilities.

Players will use anything against you when they have not played well. It's because the pillow was too hard. We've travelled too far. The hotel wasn't right. My pasta wasn't cooked enough. The lesser lights in particular, the weaker characters, will all be looking for an excuse if things go wrong, so make sure you don't give them one.

My own experience with Scotland is that preparation matters, but you still have to perform on the pitch whether it's good or bad.

Neither Argentina 1978 nor Mexico 1986 were exactly triumphs of forward planning on our part, but we got it right at Spain in 1982 yet still didn't progress.

● ● ●

My first taste of international football came when I was selected for the Scotland squad of 40 before the 1974 World Cup tournament but missed the cut when it was whittled down to 22. Scotland played West Germany in Frankfurt prior to the World Cup and I was in the squad for that game. I was 20 then and it was the first time Kenny Dalglish and I had roomed together.

He hadn't seen a hairdryer before and thought I was a bit effeminate using one, so decided to give me a wide berth. I was in my bed thinking, 'Where is he, I thought he was supposed to be a really good pro? It's after midnight, he must be out somewhere, he's a right stop out.' But Kenny was hiding, waiting for me to go to sleep, so he could sneak into his own bed.

I remember the Adidas man there was giving away equipment and we all got £100 for wearing their boots in the game. When you think of that now, £100 a game from Adidas to wear their boots! I didn't play, but still received the fee.

I can't remember feeling nervy or inferior in the company of guys like Billy Bremner and Denis Law. I never suffered from an inferiority complex. It was the same when I walked into the Liverpool dressing room. It wasn't, 'Wow, this is the big time.' I walked in and felt I should be in the team. That's the way I was.

At Tottenham, I thought I should have been in the team ahead of Steve Perryman, Alan Mullery and Martin Peters. That's how I always was.

I made my debut in a friendly against East Germany at Hampden in October 1974, played in a European Championship qualifier against Spain there the following month, then a friendly away to Sweden in April 1975, but after that I dropped off Scotland's radar for nearly three years and I wasn't involved in the qualification campaign for Argentina.

I was doing well at Middlesbrough, so it's surprising nobody noticed that. I moved to Liverpool in January 1978, and by February against Bulgaria at Hampden I was back in the Scotland team. Liverpool had watched me for a while before they signed me. I couldn't get in the Scottish team back then, but I could get into the team that had just won the European Cup? Someone wasn't doing their job properly.

Scotland were never going to win the World Cup in Argentina, as the famous Andy Cameron song, 'Ally's Tartan Army' suggested, but we had a strong team going into that tournament.

As a nation, we don't need much encouragement to start shouting from the rooftops but it should have been the opposite way, of simply saying we were going there to do our best. I remember going to Hampden and there were 30,000 people just to see us off to the airport before we drove down to Prestwick to fly out to Argentina.

We were all put under extreme pressure by the hype. No European team had won a World Cup in South America until Germany did in 2014. Were we really going to be the first?

It wasn't professional. It was the exact opposite of what I was used to at Liverpool, where if we won, it was all about, 'It was our day today we enjoyed the luck, next time it could be very different.' That was the schooling I'd had at Liverpool.

At that World Cup with Scotland, it couldn't have been any more different. It was, 'We're going to win it, we're a great team, we've got great players, we'll show everyone.' It couldn't have been more foreign to how we did things at Anfield. It was a real sea change in terms of attitude.

Doing a lap of honour before we had even kicked a ball? It put the whole nation on edge, with everyone believing. It was absurd. Remember, I'd not taken part in the qualification, so I was there but I was taking a back seat. It was not my party.

The drive down to Prestwick, with grandchildren, grandparents, with the Scottish flags on the side of the dual carriageway all the way down to the airport, is the memory I prefer to treasure. That was spontaneous, not stage-managed, and how it should have been, but the whole nation had been whipped up, so it could only end one way and that was in disappointment.

I never blamed manager Ally MacLeod for staying loyal to the players who had got him to the finals in Argentina. He was a really lovely human being, but that job, and the pressures that came with it, were too much for him. Now that I have been a manager myself, I understand it better and I don't think that was the right job for him.

You couldn't have got it any more wrong than Scotland did in Argentina. We stayed half an hour from Cordoba, where our first two group games were to be played, in the Sierras Hotel near Alta Gracia. The omens were bad from the start when the clutch burned out on the bus taking us there. The swimming pool lacked one essential ingredient – water. The gardeners and even some waiters carried machine guns to protect us and there was a temporary wire fence between us and an adjoining casino, which may either have been to keep trespassers out or keep us in.

It wasn't Ally MacLeod's fault that the security at our hotel was claustrophobic and we were bored. Denis Howell, the sports minister, turned up to see us one day and I got talking to one of his security team who was a Scouser, a special forces guy. I asked him, 'How good is our security here?' and he just started laughing.

The hotel rooms were not the best. The training ground wasn't handy and its surface wasn't great, and then there was the whole thing with Willie Johnston and the failed drug test.

Willie tested positive for a banned substance called fencamfamine after our opening match, a 3–1 defeat to Peru. The stimulant had been part of the Reactivan tablets he had been taking for his hayfever. We had all been well warned beforehand by the doctor to declare anything we were on, so there was no excuse and he was sent home.

We started well enough in that match, taking the lead through Joe Jordan's goal after a good passing move, but Peru equalised two minutes before half-time through Cesar Cueto. Don Masson missed a penalty for us at the start of the second half before Teofilo Cubillas, their experienced playmaker, scored twice, the second from a swerving free-kick.

We underestimated them. Playing a South American team in South America is never easy, no matter who it is. It doesn't have to be one of the big guns, an Argentina or Brazil. Playing any of them there is difficult and we came unstuck and then the mood in the camp, all the optimism, just drifted away overnight.

The next game was against Iran and we had to win it. Everyone thought it would be a formality, but it wasn't. I remember being in the dugout with 10 to 15 minutes to go. It was one of those dugouts that was sunk into the ground. We were 1–0 down and Ally was looking along the line to see who he could put on to make changes. He was to our right, but every time he looked in our direction, everyone immediately swivelled to the left.

The players didn't want to catch his eye. We didn't want to go on for the closing stages of what turned out to be a dire 1–1 draw. After the game, there was a ramp above our bus, where the Scottish supporters had gathered and they were not happy. They were shouting and screaming at us. It was quite aggressive, strong abuse.

I didn't play in those first two games. I had gone to Argentina behind Bruce Rioch, Archie Gemmill and Don Masson in the midfield pecking order, and rightly so because they had played really well to get us there.

I finally came in for the Holland match, which we won 3–2 and we played much better. We came back from conceding a penalty converted by Rob Rensenbrink to equalise through Kenny. Then we took the lead at the start of the second half when I was pushed in the box and Archie Gemmill scored from the spot. He then scored the goal of the tournament, a marvellous dribble through the Dutch defence. There were 20 minutes left and one more goal would have put us through, but instead Johnny Rep scored from long range for them to put us out.

As the recriminations started, with several players selling their stories to the papers, I headed for the beach in Rio. I was lying there, when I read in the *Observer* that Archie Gemmill had described me as a 'chocolate soldier'. As in, 'If he was chocolate, he would eat himself.' He was 100 per cent correct. That was me as a young man, supremely self-confident. I should also point out that in a squad infamous for its perms, mine was natural. I just had curly hair, for the record.

● ● ●

If Argentina was a farce, then Spain 1982 was completely different. The contrast between Ally MacLeod and Jock Stein, who succeeded him, couldn't have been greater. I was talking with Hugh McIlvanney one Christmas and I said to him, 'Alright then, there's a lunch taking place and there's Alex Ferguson, Matt Busby, Bill Shankly and Jock Stein – who is the dominant one at that table?' Without hesitation, he said, 'Stein.'

That confirmed what I already thought: that it wasn't imaginary, it wasn't in my head. That was how other football people saw Jock Stein. He'd won the European Cup with Celtic and everything in Scotland. He was held in such high regard and had quite an abrasive manner and also a physical presence. He walked into a room and it would suddenly go quiet.

He liked me, but he would also be harder on me than anybody else. He saw that I could deal with it and that the message he was sending out to the rest of the group was being noted. 'I can have a go at him, he's my captain, he's captain of Liverpool, he's Billy big bollocks, but I can nail him, so the rest of you be careful.' I respected and responded to that. I could easily have played for him if he'd been my club manager. He would have got the best out of me.

I remember one game in Belgium where Kenny and I went out shopping and came back late for a team meeting because we had the wrong time for it. Jock berated us in the reception of the hotel. When he was finished, I thought, 'I'm glad that's over.'

Then, as we were walking to where the rest of them were waiting for us – and that walk from the reception seemed like a mile along all those corridors – he was still abusing us. Then, when you thought that was it, we got in the room and he repeated it again.

So we got it three times because he was making the point in front of the rest of the players: these two big heads, who do they think they are keeping you waiting? When I went into management, that's how I would have dealt with it, too. The rest of the players had to see he was treating everyone the same, even these two big heads from Liverpool.

When Jock asked me to captain Scotland during the 1982 World Cup in Spain, it meant so much to me. Apart from the honour itself, it's the guy who has a choice from several strong candidates and picks you that means so much. The great Jock Stein, someone who had been around top men all of their football life, choosing you to be his captain. That was special.

Everything was far more professional under him. It was four years on, with someone who was a strong disciplinarian in charge. Nobody was taking any advantages with Jock Stein. There was no grand send-off this time, just us slipping quietly out of Scotland to a top hotel in the Algarve to finish our preparations before settling into our tournament base at Sotogrande in southern Spain. Nobody could get in and out without Jock's say so, although he did allow Sean Connery to come along with us to watch Brazil beat the USSR 2–1 in the opening game in our group.

I can't remember any negative stuff getting out. We had the most wonderful training facility. It was a polo field but had a magnificent surface. The hotel we stayed in was good. The only mishap I recall was Kenny sitting on a glass table and going right through it, resulting in splinters in his famous backside.

We conceded two sloppy goals in our first game against New Zealand and won 5–2 when it should have been 5–0. Then we faced Tele Santana's Brazil, still the best team to have never won a World Cup in my view. It must have been 100 degrees fahrenheit inside that stadium in Seville when we went out to 'warm up'. We came back in and put our heads under the shower, before putting our playing strips on and coming out to line up for the national anthems.

As the anthems were being played, I could see to my right the linesmen and the referee and then Socrates, Brazil's captain, alongside the whole Brazilian team who looked like they had just stepped out of a shop display window.

Then I looked left at our lads, and they were covered in sweat as if they had just finished 90 minutes. I thought there and then, 'We're in trouble today.' I turned back to the front, glanced towards the main stand and there were all these semi-naked Brazilian women, waving and swooning over their players, and there we were, pasty white northern Europeans. It must have been quite a contrast.

We made the mistake of scoring first through Dave Narey's goal. It was like pulling a lion's tail. We woke them up, they found another gear, and we chased the ball for the next 70 minutes or so, not getting a kick and conceding four goals.

That Brazil team had some wonderful footballers like Socrates, Falcao, Junior and Eder, but Zico was the best of them by a country mile. He was untouchable. A big part of the game back then involved trying to mess your opponent around physically to see if they fancied it. The two players in my career who I never laid a finger on were Zico and Alan Ball. They just had this ability to sense where you were, where you were coming from, and would just pop the ball off before you got within a yard of them.

Besides the two goals we conceded against New Zealand, we shipped too many against Brazil, and that left us requiring a win in our final match against the USSR. Bear in mind that they were drawing from a population of 150 million, and some of their best players came from countries that are now independent, like Georgia and Ukraine, while we were a nation of five million. We didn't have enough to beat them, but we gave a good account of ourselves until a mix-up between Willie Miller and Alan Hansen put the match beyond us and my late goal was only a consolation in a 2–2 draw.

We were the nearly-men again and that's the story of Scotland at the World Cup. To compare with the Liverpool teams that I played in, were they all brilliant players? No. Did they have any obvious weaknesses? No. The worst player would be a seven out of ten. But on a bad day, Scotland would have players at less than that. That was the difference.

● ● ●

At Mexico in 1986, I never recovered from my first meal there. We prepared before the tournament in the USA, but when we got to Mexico itself the hotel was substandard. The first time we sat down for food, I ordered an omelette, which turned up with some bread. There were some little speckles on the bread, courtesy of a chicken out the back. After that, I was living on bars of chocolate that the staff had brought with them.

Not only did we get our accommodation wrong again but we also made mistakes in our preparation for altitude, although we were not alone in that. I always found playing at altitude difficult. I was usually a good trainer, I looked after myself and considered myself one of the fitter members of the group, but when we went with Scotland a couple of years earlier to Canada and played at altitude, I found that really difficult, too.

There are several trains of thought on how to prepare to play at altitude and the thinking now is different from what it was then. When you go to altitude everyone's different but it's a slow, progressive thing over 10 days to two weeks, where your body is gradually losing power, diminishing in its capability to perform. After about two weeks, you are at your lowest point, then you start to recover, and then it's another couple of weeks and you're ready for it.

The theory is that for every 1000 feet you are going to perform at, you have to spend a week preparing at that level. So for 7000 feet above sea level, which we were playing at in Mexico, we should have been away for seven weeks. More importantly, we did what we shouldn't have done because your body is being driven down for two weeks and is at its lowest point. That's when we left our altitude training camp in Santa Fe to go to Mexico to play games.

So you either do the seven weeks at 7000 feet or you do what Germany did at the 2010 World Cup in South Africa. They stayed at sea level, where their body condition was normal, and then flew in, played the game and got out of there before the altitude started to run their bodies down. I personally struggled and it was nothing to do with my heart problems later on.

Ironically, the benefit of being at altitude for four or five weeks kicked in after the World Cup when I came back to Rangers. I was 33 by then but absolutely flying in pre-season. The younger lads were looking at me in amazement, because I was at the front of every group when we doing the running. It proved that Scotland had got it all wrong in Mexico.

It didn't help that we were in the so-called 'Group of Death' with Denmark, West Germany and Uruguay. We were unlucky to lose 1–0 to a really good Danish team with Preben Elkjaer and Michael Laudrup in attack. Against West Germany, Gordon Strachan gave us the lead, but we wilted in the heat and altitude and lost 2–1. I really struggled in those conditions.

I can remember going down on my haunches during the game and thinking, 'God, do I not feel good.' It was the worst I'd ever felt on a football pitch. I couldn't breathe. It must have been 80 to 90 degrees Fahrenheit. We were at 7000 feet above sea level, and I had lost a stone of my normal playing weight, so it shouldn't have been a surprise.

We'd lost to two really good teams, but still had a chance of sneaking through to the last 16 going into the third game against Uruguay. If there was a game for me, that was it. I was 33, I had all my experience in European football and had just spent the last two years playing in a Latin country.

It was made for me, but Alex Ferguson, who had taken over as Scotland manager after Jock Stein's death during our decisive qualifier in Wales, left me out. It was the one and only time I was dropped in my career, but I couldn't disagree because I knew I hadn't played well and I wasn't physically right either.

It must have been difficult for Fergie, given that I was captain and about to become the Rangers manager who would challenge his Aberdeen side's dominance in Scotland. He was very respectful and I offered no argument, but with hindsight I think he's admitted he made a mistake. He could have left me out of the West Germany game to have me ready for Uruguay. We drew that final game 0–0. They had a player sent off in the first minute of the match, for a foul on Gordon Strachan, and played almost 90 minutes with 10 men, so that was another nearly story to add to the list.

After that game I announced I would be retiring from international football. I knew I was about to become player-manager at Rangers and that I wouldn't be around for the next World Cup anyway. It just would have been too much with everything I had on my hands at Ibrox.

I finished with 54 caps for Scotland but would have had more if I'd played in more friendlies. I missed many of them and that was down to Bob Paisley. He would say, dismissively, 'They don't mean anything.'

Kenny finished with 102 caps, but he had a chance to go back to Glasgow to see his family around the friendlies. It was different for me, coming from Edinburgh. After the game, you had to get back down the road, so there wasn't the same chance for me to see my family. Maybe that's not a great reason, but that's the reality.

There was also an element of the Anglo players never being fully accepted. If you don't play for Rangers or Celtic, you are deemed to be not quite Scottish, or have betrayed them a wee bit if you have gone to play in England. I reckon that was caused by the television coverage when we played. It's not like today, where you can watch live games every weekend from every league.

Scotland supporters would see the highlights on a Saturday night, watching the guys based in England excelling for their clubs, and it was like, 'They not doing as well or the same for Scotland.' I couldn't understand it at the time, but I get it now, particularly having worked at Rangers and seen the passion they have for their own players.

I also understood what Bob meant about friendlies when I later became a manager myself. I thought it was an ideal opportunity to go and look at players that you might fancy signing, but it was a waste of time. I soon stopped going because you are seeing players at 90 per cent, they are not at it, and the guys they are playing against are taking it easy, too, so you can't judge a player in that environment.

It was a bit like when I was manager of Rangers and would see someone playing against us and think, 'He's a player, I'll keep an eye on him.' Then you would go and watch him the next week and he'd be a yard off the pace, with no aggression in him. When people played Rangers, and it must have been the same for Celtic, it was like their cup final. They were full of aggression. They either wanted to play for Rangers because they had been boyhood Rangers supporters, or they were Celtic supporters who wanted to beat you. I quickly worked that out in Scotland.

I do understand, because I've been a manager, that you have to get your team together somehow. Do you do that and not play a friendly, that's the question. The football associations want the friendlies because there's money involved, but what does the manager get out of it? I don't think it's what he finds out about players in the 90 minutes, because they are not at it. In a team gathering he'll find out how they interact with each other, who the characters are, who you can totally rely on. I think he will get more of that from these get-togethers than from 90 minutes of phoney war on the pitch.

There has to be qualifiers, because that's part and parcel of the game. Anyone can beat anyone else at any given time. That's the way it has always been and there's even more chance of that now, when you look at what Iceland did in the Euros after qualifying at Holland's expense.

Iceland's players are not top level, but they are out there, across Europe, playing in professional leagues, living and training like the guys at the top end of the Premier League. So those guys, even if they are playing for lesser countries, are every bit as fit, prepared and motivated as the big guys and deserve their shot at reaching a finals tournament.

I hope Scotland will reach one again soon, too. It has been too long now.

7

REVIVING RANGERS

As a boy going to Ibrox as a supporter on several European nights, I thought I was aware of how big Glasgow Rangers were. Then as a player I won things at the highest level with Liverpool, and played in three World Cups for Scotland. Yet despite all that, there was very little to prepare me for joining Rangers.

I was offered the job of player-manager at Rangers in the spring of 1986 when I was still 32. David Holmes, the managing director, flew out to Milan and I drove from Genoa to meet him at Linate airport. He persuaded me within half an hour that it would be a great job for me. Although I was in the latter stages of my playing career and I'd never given management a thought, as I drove home I became more and more excited by the idea of it.

People compared it to Kenny Dalglish becoming Liverpool's player-manager a year earlier, but there was an enormous difference. Kenny took over a team that had won the European Cup 12 months before and just been beaten in the final that season. I was taking over a team that hadn't won the league for eight years. I was starting from scratch. There was no foundation in place. Although we were both player-managers, the job descriptions were very different.

I was naive and braver than a lion. The thought of doing all that today would frighten me to death, but back then I had no fear, I thought I could take anything on. After all, my playing career had more or less been on a continual upward curve, other than when I was 19 and Tottenham sold me to Middlesbrough.

As a young man, you think you are invincible. For the first year at Rangers, I was playing on a Saturday, finishing at a quarter to five before racing to Glasgow airport to catch a flight to Majorca, where my family were living at the time. It was leaving at six. I'd spend Sunday with them and then fly back on the Monday, missing training. I'd maybe play in a midweek game and then play at the weekend again.

As well as training and trying to stay fit as a player, I was also doing the manager's job, travelling up and down to England to look at players or maybe to Europe on occasion, so I took a hell of a lot on. People forget, I had just turned 33 when I started that job. I hear people today say someone's a young manager at 45 or 46, still learning their way. Really?

When I joined Rangers, the club already had a brand new stadium in place, as a result of the Ibrox Disaster. That tragedy occurred on Saturday, 2 January 1971, when 66 people were killed following the collapse of crush barriers as supporters tried to leave the stadium at the same time.

The new Ibrox had a capacity of 44,000, which meant that Rangers had the best and safest stadium in Britain by the time I arrived. We could pay the same wages and match the transfer fees of any of the big English clubs, who were by then rebuilding their own stadiums on the back of the Taylor Report, after the 1989 Hillsborough disaster, and were also banned from Europe after the Heysel tragedy four years earlier.

I also had tremendous support from David Holmes and Lawrence Marlborough, the club owner, to begin with and then David Murray later on when he bought the club. I was basically allowed to run the whole football side of things at Rangers.

With hindsight, I didn't know how well off I was. In my very first job in management, I eventually became a director and the second largest shareholder at the club. Without realising it, I was in an extremely strong position then.

Those circumstances and some serious salesmanship allowed me to reverse the tradition of the best Scottish players moving to England. Instead, England internationals moved north of the border to join us. It was a market I knew well.

A lot of the players that I brought up to Scotland were ones whom

I'd played against and, in some cases, alongside. Rangers and Celtic, historically, buy players from other Scottish clubs and there's a premium to be paid, while the ones that don't work out generally go back at a discount. I reasoned that if I bought players from England and it didn't work out, there was a far better resale market for them.

Signing Terry Butcher from Ipswich Town was the catalyst for everything that followed. He was England captain at the time and regarded as the best centre-half in Britain. We landed him and then everything became possible.

Terry had reservations about joining. He was playing for a World XI in Los Angeles and I'd arranged to meet him at the Sheraton at Heathrow when he flew back, because I knew that Tottenham and Manchester United were also interested in him. He promised he'd meet me, but because there were two Sheratons at Heathrow, I thought he'd done a runner.

I was in one and phoned the other and got the concierge, who said, 'Yes, there's a Mr Butcher in reception here.' I couldn't tell him who I was because we were still keeping it quiet. I eventually got Terry up the road and all his chat was, 'What will the supporters think of me?'

The warm reception he got from them on the steps of Ibrox allayed all his fears on that front, and it was then a very simple job to sign him. In the beginning, before the English influx really got going, there was a need for a bit of selling Rangers to players, but once I got Terry signed it was a very easy sell to everyone else that followed him.

Before Terry arrived, I'd managed to sign Chris Woods from Nottingham Forest for £600,000. I hadn't forgotten him from the League Cup final of 1978, my first year at Liverpool. I wasn't eligible to play and it finished 0–0 at Wembley before Forest won the replay 1–0 at Old Trafford. I remembered thinking then what a good young goalkeeper he was and kept an eye on his career after that.

He was considered the long-term replacement for Peter Shilton as England goalkeeper at that point. With him and Terry on board, I had the start of the spine of my side. Next, Graham Roberts arrived from Tottenham for £450,000 to reinforce it further.

I'd wanted to sign Richard Gough from the start, but Dundee United refused to sell him to another Scottish club, so I had wait over a year to bring him back to Scotland from Tottenham. I'd admired Richard as a Scotland colleague for his professionalism and leadership qualities and was certain he would set standards for the other Rangers players to follow. That was proved correct when he later captained the club on its run to nine consecutive titles.

We signed good professionals and winners as the revolution continued. Some worked out and some didn't, but they all played a part of some kind in our success.

There were classy, established England internationals like Ray Wilkins, Trevor Francis and Mark Hateley. There were also players who were perhaps not international class but were still good, solid professionals, rated highly enough in England that they could be sold back there if they didn't settle in Scotland or fit into our team permanently.

Guys like Kevin Drinkell, Nigel Spackman, Mark Falco, Mel Sterland and Terry Hurlock came into this category and all did well for me.

Bigger money went on Gary Stevens and Trevor Steven, who had formed such an impressive right flank in the strong Everton team of the mid-1980s and also went on to do so for England at the 1986 World Cup in Mexico. Gary came first, in 1988 for £1.25 million, with Trevor following a year after for £1.7 million, before he was later sold to Marseille for £5 million.

Gary was a tremendous athlete and rarely injured, while Trevor was a clever midfielder who could play wide or centrally. They were the best English players in their positions at the time, which shows the pull Rangers had by then.

Although I thought I knew a lot about football because of the level I had played at and the success I'd had, being thrown into management was another step up altogether. I was very lucky that David Holmes gave me carte blanche to succeed at the club.

Appointing Walter Smith as my assistant was also of paramount importance as I started out in management. We were first thrown together for Scotland's 1986 World Cup preparations. After Jock Stein's death, Walter was part of Fergie's coaching team that went to Mexico. He'd learnt the management side of things from Jim McLean at Dundee United and we just hit it off and are still the best of pals.

I was very lucky because he was experienced in management and our personalities just suited each other. I'm not suggesting Walter was a pussycat, but he was more of a sensible head whereas I was a little excitable and still trying to play. I would trust Walter with my life and I quickly realised that.

I was the face of the club, but he was as important to the cause as I was. I was way too gung-ho back then and went looking for trouble as a young man, whereas Walter would be more likely to stand back and be more thoughtful, although he also could explode when he felt he had to be like that.

I never really gelled with a guy called Alan Montgomery, who had come in from Scottish Television as chief executive to increase revenue through sponsorship deals and so on. He began to interfere in the football side to my irritation. I made it clear I couldn't work with the man and he left the club.

In contrast, Walter and I were a perfect fit, very good for each other. He warned me to expect a hot reception on my debut at Hibs, but his advice was wasted and Fleet Street's finest headed north to see me sent off in my first game, for kicking George McCluskey during a confrontation in the centre circle at Easter Road.

I took plenty of stick for my red card, but the silver lining was that my team stood behind me to a man that day. They all wanted to be involved, which was fabulous. It was my own stupid fault, but their reaction was the one you would want. It said, 'Alright, he's made a fool of himself, but we're all in it together.'

I fully understood the reaction to my arrival at Rangers. Here was me turning up, having never played football in Scotland, as Billy big nuts, coming from Italy to show them how it's done. I get that. I was arrogant and I understand why people didn't like me. It was born out of my confidence, youthfulness and an inner belief that wouldn't be shaken.

It was the right thing for the club at that time. Rangers are an institution. They are no ordinary football club, just as Celtic are no ordinary football club. They are abnormal in the context of Scottish football, too big to be there with the size of support they have. It's all out of proportion and the Scottish way is, 'We'll show the big guy that he's not so big.' I quickly accepted that and we dealt with it.

You rarely get a big job because everything in the garden is rosy or because it's all a good news story. There's usually some sort of tweaking to do, or something more is required. In Rangers' case, it was more than that, it was a complete rebuilding job, but, within three years, we were the dominant team north of the border.

Fergie staying or not staying at Aberdeen wouldn't have mattered. Maybe he knew that when he moved to Manchester United in November 1986, although that's a job I am sure he would have taken whatever the circumstances. If you are offered the United job, you are going to take it, no matter who turns up on your doorstep.

Aberdeen had dominated under Fergie before my arrival in April 1986 and his departure for Old Trafford seven months later, and they were at least as big a rival to us as Celtic in the early days. We had some real battles with them, the most notorious one perhaps at Pittodrie in October 1988.

In one particularly fraught passage of play, the whistle went and

Ian Durrant took his eye off the ball just as Neil Simpson, the Aberdeen midfielder, came in and caught him late. I still believe it wouldn't have happened if the whistle hadn't gone, because Durrant was one of those players with a sixth sense of what was coming, but he thought the game had stopped and sustained a serious knee injury as a consequence.

I also had problems with a calf injury that I picked up in another match against Aberdeen, although I stress there was no malice involved in mine. I kept breaking down because I wouldn't allow it to heal properly and it eventually ended my playing career.

Terry Butcher also broke his leg against Aberdeen in 1987 and that injury, I remain convinced, was the main reason that Celtic responded to us lifting the league in my first season with a league and Scottish Cup double in 1987–88, their centenary season, under Billy McNeill, who had replaced Davie Hay as their manager.

I am not complaining about it, but though many wanted us to be successful at Rangers, there were twice as many wanting me to fail. It was a case of living with that, and because of my attitude and personality I could deal with it.

For example, I went to the Glasgow Cup final against Celtic at Hampden one year. I had a black three-quarter-length leather coat on and a black roll-neck jumper underneath, so I must have looked like something from a Milk Tray advert. It was effectively the reserve sides of the two clubs, but there were still about 40,000 people there.

As I was standing talking to someone outside, out of the corner of my eye I saw a kid being dragged towards me by his dad until they stood about two yards away from me. Then the dad pointed at me and said, 'There you are, son, there's the bad man.' So in his house, when I came on the telly, I was 'the bad man'. The kid was pulling away from his dad as he said this. It made me chuckle at the time, but afterwards it made me quite sad.

That antipathy towards me lasted for the whole time I was there. A lot of that was due to the size and spending power of Rangers and the momentum behind the club. People in England struggle to comprehend how big Rangers and Celtic are in Scotland. You just have to look at it in recent years, with Rangers playing in the lower leagues and still getting full houses playing against semi-professional teams.

Where else would that happen? Possibly at Celtic. Possibly at Manchester United. Possibly at Liverpool. But nowhere else.

● ● ●

When Rangers went into administration and liquidation in 2012, not only did it damage them, it damaged Scottish football in general. While they spent four years playing in the lower leagues before returning to the top tier, Celtic stagnated and only really got going again under Brendan Rodgers in 2016–17. They raised their game to win an unbeaten treble after Rangers beat them in the Scottish Cup semi-final the previous season, and they deserve great credit for that.

The gloating at Rangers' demise was predictable, but also parochial.

I'm not saying that it would have been any different had the roles been reversed – Rangers supporters would have reacted the same way – but it was the wrong reaction and it was the wrong decision to demote them in 2012. I wonder if all the people who voted for that would do so if they had their time again. If they say 'yes', then they don't have Scottish football at heart.

I tried my best to make Scottish football less parochial and it saddens me that its profile has diminished so much in recent years. If they were on a level playing field financially with Chelsea, Manchester City, Manchester United, Tottenham, Liverpool and Arsenal, and if they had the same income from television, Rangers and Celtic would be in the Champions League and would have the same standard of players as the big English clubs. If they were playing in the Premier League, they would be challenging to win it within a decade.

I look back now at my time at Ibrox and think, 'Would I have done it differently?' The answer is probably not. We became the best in Scotland within three years. Maybe I was too aggressive or arrogant on occasion, but every young man looks back on certain things and thinks, 'Maybe that wasn't the best thing to do.'

I like to think that it was needed, that I gave all the players a bit of confidence that wasn't there before, because I was on the pitch with them as well, and there was a belief that we would not be beaten in the bigger picture. 'Yes, we'll lose a few games, but we'll get there over time.'

Sometimes with Celtic and Rangers, it was about more than just the football. When I was appointed as Rangers manager, I was asked if I would ever sign a Catholic. I replied, 'Of course, I would.' I could see all the press men raise their eyes to the sky, like they had heard it all before, but I meant it.

My wife, at the time, was a Catholic, my kids had been christened Catholic, so it was not an issue for me and I proved that by signing Maurice Johnston from Nantes in 1989 when Celtic thought he was about to join them.

I'd previously tried to sign Ray Houghton and John Collins, but had failed to persuade them. It was ridiculous. As Celtic's manager, Jock Stein always said he could concentrate his efforts on promising Protestants. Given that Scotland is split 50–50, you were limiting yourself to picking from 50 per cent of the kids that were out there.

It looked like Celtic had signed Maurice, until one day I made a passing remark to Bill McMurdo, his agent, in the grand entrance foyer at Ibrox. As I walked down the marble staircase there, he was leaning against the radiator at the bottom of it.

'You should have let us know about Maurice, we would have been in for him,' I said, and then kept walking.

Immediately, Bill was on my shoulder. 'Do you really mean it?' 'Yes,' I replied.

That's how it all started. Next we ran the idea past David Murray. David became owner of Rangers in November 1988, after I heard that Lawrence Marlborough was looking to sell up from David Holmes and mentioned it to him. He was interested in buying Ayr United because he'd grown up there and I said, 'What are you thinking about, when you could buy Rangers?'

Walter Smith and I drove to his office at The Gyle in Edinburgh to raise the idea of signing Maurice. David puffed his cheeks out, then after 30 seconds there was an expletive and then a 'Yeah, let's do it.'

There was some resistance within the club, with other directors feeling that the fans would desert us in droves in protest, but I argued that very quickly Maurice would win the right-minded majority over with his industry, football and goalscoring, and I was proved right on that score. The bottom line was that I had played for Scotland with him, knew his qualities, and his flaws, but rated him as a player.

I am proud of it, but I don't dwell on it now. Was it a good thing? That's for history to decide. I believe it was, if you reflect on the players the club have signed since then who have gone on to become legends. So I look back on the Maurice Johnston signing with pride, but I also see it as something that would have happened eventually anyway. It's now taken for granted that Rangers will sign Catholic players and little comment is made when they do so. It has changed so much for the better on that score at the club, so I am glad that I brought that ridiculous unwritten rule that was holding the club back to a spectacular end.

Maurice probably deserves most of the credit for taking on something that others rejected because it would bring too much grief. He stayed out of Glasgow to avoid any trouble there and we provided a bodyguard for him to stop any idiots, from either side of the divide, confronting him. I admire his courage in taking it on, because he was the one in the spotlight, playing in the games and taking the stick, sometimes from both sides.

The actual deal had to be done discreetly, of course. I flew to Charles de Gaulle airport in Paris and Bill McMurdo used Orly airport there, so that we wouldn't be spotted together. We then met at a little cafe in Paris to agree the details over coffee.

We unveiled Maurice at Ibrox and then immediately took him out to Tuscany, where the rest of the squad were in their pre-season training camp, to let things die down a bit. I dealt firmly with players in the squad who refused to welcome him to the club, making it clear they wouldn't be staying.

The knock-on effect of us signing Maurice demoralised Celtic. He'd come back from Nantes for a few days in Glasgow, there was a photograph taken with Billy McNeill, Celtic's manager, and he was going back to sign for them. Next thing, he's our player. It damaged them. It prevented them from signing one of the best Scottish players around at the time, so we weakened them, but the psychological damage lasted for years afterwards.

It wasn't just Maurice Johnston. We signed Mark Walters, Rangers' first black player for 50 years, and the late Avi Cohen, who was Jewish, too. I'd spent my adult life in England and had my eyes opened to a lot more than if I'd stayed at home and not gone 'abroad'. Signing someone who was a different religion or different colour felt completely normal. It wasn't an issue. It improved

Rangers then and allowed them to grow as a football club after that.

Not that it was always plain sailing being Maurice's manager. His behaviour and form in his first season were exemplary, but things started to go wrong as we prepared for his second season, once more at a training camp in Tuscany.

I had two of my kids over because I was separated at the time, so they had come to visit and I had said to Walter to let the players have a drink that night. I was in my bed and I could hear a commotion going on, but I chose to ignore it and let Walter deal with it. When I came down in the morning, Maurice looked like he had been in a fight with a Bengal tiger. His face was all scratched and bloodied. I asked Walter what happened to Maurice and he said there had been an argument between him and Mark Hateley, who we had signed that summer from Monaco.

I don't think they exchanged blows, there would only have been one winner there, but someone had been into Maurice's room and taken the mattress off his bed and it was one of the old-fashioned metal spring ones, so when he came in after a few beers and his argument with Mark, he'd dived onto the bed face first and it was like a cheese grater on his skin.

Mark eventually took over from Maurice as Ally McCoist's partner, although their first season was when all three were at the club and Ally, the darling of the crowd for his goals and endearing personality, occasionally found himself on the bench. Of all the players I had at

Rangers, he was probably the one I was fondest of, because he could reduce me to tears of laughter even when I was trying to have a row with him in my office.

The charisma that would later make him such a success on *A Question of Sport* was apparent from our first pre-season together. We were in a wine bar, when Ally grabbed a beer bottle and launched into a Bruce Springsteen number to a rapt German audience. It took about another half an hour for his impromptu 'concert' to come to an end.

I appreciated Ally's gifts as a finisher, but felt I needed to keep on his case to get the best out of him. He christened himself 'The Judge' during his period on the bench, and his teammates called him 'Dudley' after I said he was 'a dud' in one sharp dressing room exchange.

● ● ●

A deal that might even have topped the signing of Maurice Johnston as a sensation was almost done that same year, 1989. It could have led to me becoming Manchester United manager, replacing Alex Ferguson, as Michael Knighton tried to finance a takeover at Old Trafford. One evening in David's office in Edinburgh, we met him and thrashed out a deal in which David would put down £10 million to help him buy Martin Edwards' shares.

I was going to manage United and Walter was going to stay and manage Rangers. I went to bed believing that was the case. The formal meeting finished at 10pm then David, Michael Knighton and I went to David's house and Louise, his late wife, made bacon and eggs for us, but David woke up the next morning and changed his mind because there was a lot of controversy at the time about people owning two clubs in different countries. I had no doubts, though. If the deal had been done, I would have been up for managing Manchester United and handing the reins at Rangers to Walter.

Perhaps that was an early sign that I'd had my fill of all the antagonism in Scotland. The club had become a bit of a monster and, looking back, I was not blameless in that, falling out with sections of the press, with TV people and with my own players through my confrontational style. Without sounding big-headed, I'd become the most famous person in Scotland at that time. Looking back, I suppose it did tickle my ego.

I had been well-known or famous in football terms for a number of years, I had a certain profile, but in that time at Rangers it went to a completely different level, where you could end up on the front pages at any moment for one misdemeanour, and that was what ultimately made me leave the place. It became more about me and trying to get me off the front pages, than what the 11 lads on the football pitch were doing.

I was banned from the touchline and then Scottish Television caught me on camera as I popped my head out the tunnel and couldn't get the attention of Walter at Ibrox one day. They must have literally lifted the camera off its legs to get the top of my head when

I edged down the tunnel to shout to Walter to change something, but I ended up getting another ban for it.

People were after me all the time because I was the story. It was stupid of me to give them the chance to do that, but in the same breath they were turning round and wanting you to be helpful when they were making life as difficult for you as possible.

I get all that now. That's the media, and I understand that now I am part of it. I'd do it all very differently today. You come back to Jock Stein's saying of 'never go looking for an argument when you're a manager, it will come to you', and it certainly did at Rangers.

The STV incident also led to me falling out with Terry Butcher, who, as I have made clear, was my key signing at the start of reviving Rangers. As I felt my ban was down to the STV cameras, I banned our players from talking to them.

Terry ignored that ban, after I dropped him because he was having some knee trouble. I could see him from my office at Ibrox talking to Jim White, now of Sky Sports, but then at STV. A newspaper article followed and I was furious.

It saddened me because he was the catalyst for much of what we achieved at Rangers. I should probably have handled it better than I did and Terry might say the same now. It became a case of two strong-willed individuals not prepared to back down, but it shouldn't have happened like that after the superb service he had given Rangers and the roots he had put down in Scotland.

Previously, I had also fallen out with Graham Roberts, although in that case I still maintain I had little choice, after he directly challenged my authority in front of the other players. In my view he started to play to the gallery a bit too much, and believed his excellent relationship with the crowd at Rangers made him untouchable.

I was also told that he had become unpopular with some of the younger players and decided to watch out for other warning signs that he was getting too big for his boots. Matters came to a head after a defeat at home to Aberdeen, when I blamed him for their winning goal. In response, he challenged me to sell him, in front of the other players, which left me with no choice. A manager cannot back down in those circumstances or he will lose any authority he has. It took some time to move Graham on, but we eventually sold him to Chelsea for a small profit.

The cumulative effect of all this aggravation was that I eventually left Rangers to return to Liverpool in April 1991. I was offered the manager's job there twice by Peter Robinson, Liverpool's vice-chairman, and turned it down twice after Kenny resigned.

I was banned from the touchline at the time in Scotland, I was separated from my wife and I was getting followed along the M8 by journalists looking to see what I was up to in Edinburgh of an evening. It all became unbearable. The media was divided right down the middle and I just felt it wasn't helpful to the club's cause for me to remain at Rangers.

The final straw was a second argument with a lady called Aggie Moffat, who worked behind the scenes at St Johnstone and sadly died recently. To start with, it was just about players banging their boots on the floor and leaving mud on it. She thought that wasn't right, made a point of saying so, and it grew out of proportion from there.

I just hoped she could laugh about it later and that I wasn't the bad guy. I certainly laughed about it later. It was like being spoken to by my mum again, but it didn't bother me that much.

Nevertheless, as the row escalated at the time, it almost led to me assaulting Geoff Brown, St Johnstone's chairman, as he put his arm on me. A pal of mine called Ian Blyth from Edinburgh came up to that game and on the way back I said, 'That's it, I've had enough.' By that stage, I was only one wrong sentence away from exploding.

That's how I'd become. It wasn't good for me and it wasn't good for Rangers. I phoned Peter Robinson the next day and said, 'If the [Liverpool] job is still available, I'll come and talk to you.' In retrospect, I shouldn't have done that.

David Murray tried to persuade me not to leave for Liverpool when we were sitting on the wall outside my house in Edinburgh talking about it one evening. He told me to take a year off instead, to sit on the board with him and enjoy it, then I could go back as manager if I wanted to.

We'd become really close. I'd come back from Glasgow between four and five and we'd go out for an early supper in Edinburgh at six, that was our routine from Monday to Friday.

We'd done the hard work, taken the club that hadn't won the

league for eight years, had gates of 15,000 and created a monster. I like to think what I left there, although Walter Smith certainly added to it afterwards, also provided the foundations for Rangers winning nine consecutive titles to match Jock Stein's Celtic.

DECLINE OF A DYNASTY

I bumped into Phil Neville in the gym of a hotel in Barbados after Louis van Gaal replaced David Moyes as Manchester United's manager in the summer of 2014. I asked if he'd heard anything about his own situation at the club and he replied, 'I don't think I'll be staying on.'

He had been part of Moyes' backroom team at Old Trafford and I could empathise with what David had gone through after taking over from Fergie the previous year, so I said to Phil, 'It's so similar to when I took over at Liverpool. You don't want to be the first manager afterwards, you don't want to be the second one, you want to be the third or fourth one in.'

That's how I look back on my time as manager of Liverpool. That it was the right job, but came at the wrong time.

When I took over from Kenny at Anfield in April 1991, Liverpool had always had continuity and bought players in to replace others before it became obvious to outsiders they needed replacing. It was a seamless process from one trophy-winning team to the next.

At Anfield, and this is vital, they had always bought players that could spend a year looking around and learning about the club after coming in. They were not buying players to be that instant success, coming straight into the first team and being the difference between winning and losing games. They were working two and three years ahead.

I was the first manager since Bill Shankly that didn't have that luxury. I'd had an unbelievable first stint at management with Rangers. We turned them round from a team that hadn't won the league for eight years to being the dominant club in Scotland. I was there for five years and I am credited with three league championships. They didn't give me the last one, but I left in April to go to Liverpool and we were well ahead, so I think I am entitled to claim it, too.

There was the one year that we didn't win the Scottish title when I was there, 1988, but that was because we lost Terry Butcher to a broken leg and he was our captain and main man as I've already explained. After my success at Ibrox, I felt I was invincible. I felt I was up to any job.

What people often forget is that I got the Liverpool job shortly before my 38th birthday. That job, at that time, was one for an experienced, long-in-the-tooth manager, someone who had been round the block several times.

In 1985, Kenny took over a team that had won the European Cup the year before and had just been in another European Cup final, so that would suggest there was not a lot wrong with it. He became player-manager in really difficult and tragic circumstances, after Joe Fagan had resigned following the Heysel disaster, but normally you don't get a job at a big club unless there's a lot wrong with the playing staff and things have gone pear-shaped.

My period of time at Liverpool is deemed a failure, but I did win an FA Cup, and the club still hasn't won the Premier League 23 years after I left. Would I have done things differently? Yes.

I shouldn't have allowed those players who still had a bit of life in them to go when it suited them, it should have been when it suited the football club and me, but I put that down to my love and belief that Liverpool was still the place to be. I couldn't get my head round people wanting to leave Anfield and, being confident in the job I could do after Rangers, I wanted to replace them without delay.

Yet some of the ones I brought in were not good enough. That's the mistake you make when you are in a hurry and that brings us back to the comparison with United.

They brought in Marouane Fellaini in Moyes' first window because they had failed to get the players they wanted, then they bought the likes of Angel Di Maria, Bastian Schweinsteiger, Morgan Schneiderlin, Marcos Rojo, Matteo Darmian and Memphis Depay after Van Gaal arrived. They spent a load of money on players because they were forced into it.

As the manager in that situation, you have two choices. You take a gamble and splash the cash on players that are available at the time. Alternatively, you don't take a chance and you sit there and keep your powder dry until the one you really want is available, but in that period of time you could be out the door. That's the reality of the modern game, and that's what happened to David Moyes. He bought Fellaini in one window, Juan Mata in the next one, and then he was gone.

Whoever immediately followed Alex Ferguson was on a hiding to nothing from the start. Fergie's greatest achievement was to win the Premier League by 11 points with that group of players in 2013, his last year in charge. That was, arguably, his best managerial performance in his 27 years there. It disguised that there was a decline coming, just as Liverpool's last title under Kenny in 1990 did the same at Anfield before I arrived a year later.

Although we were the dominant team when I played, we always felt United only had to put three wins back-to-back and they were the new force according to the press. Anybody who played at United automatically played for their country. There was always a tendency for the media to lean towards them, and I put that down to the journalists of the day being kids when the Munich disaster happened. There was a natural affection for the club because of that.

Peter Robinson, Liverpool's secretary, always said the great fear they had was 'if that lot along the East Lancs road ever get their act together'. That's exactly what happened after they gave Fergie quite a few years to get it right. He won his first trophy after four years, the 1990 FA Cup, and his first league title after seven years.

Knocking Liverpool off their perch, to paraphrase Fergie's famous vow, would have been everyone's aim at that time. United finally got their act together, as Peter predicted they would, and Fergie was the biggest single reason for that. Bobby Charlton should also take a great deal of credit, because Fergie was under enormous pressure in the early days and it was Bobby's support behind the scenes that kept him in a job.

Although I had played for Fergie with Scotland at the 1986 World Cup, our relationship wasn't particularly close, albeit there was a mutual respect between us. We never had words when managing against each other, even at Liverpool and Manchester United, but I am sure we must have exchanged the odd stare or glance during games.

Fergie is a really nice guy when he's winning, but when he loses he can't bear it: all of us managers and ex-managers are a bit like that.

He was similar to Jock Stein. That was who he modelled himself on – being straightforward and to the point. I speak to ex-Manchester United players now and it was the same for them with Fergie as it was for me with Jock Stein. He would simplify things and put pressure on you all the time to be training properly and looking after yourself.

Like Jock, he knew everything about you and made sure he knew if there was any tragedy or any celebration in your family. He would find out what you were up to and if you were doing stuff you shouldn't have, and he would come down on you. At Liverpool, the first thing you would know about it was if you were suddenly out of the team; and then you would be told the reason, because you had been doing A, B or C.

He micromanaged United more than Bob Paisley or Joe Fagan did at Liverpool with us, partly because of the different lifestyles of some of his players compared to our generation. I think Bob and Joe knew what we got up to, but would never mention it unless it really went over the line and affected our play.

Fergie can be charming company. For example, I remember returning to Rangers to watch an Old Firm game a few years back and I bumped into him at half-time at Ibrox. I was being driven back to Manchester afterwards, but he said he was going back on a plane and could take myself and James, my youngest son, with him.

Jimmy Bell, the kit man at Rangers, had given me a ball for James and it was just the three of us on this small jet that you couldn't stand up in. Fergie spoke to James from the moment we took off to the minute we landed. James kept asking questions and Fergie said to me, 'Never stop him asking questions.'

One of James's questions was how did Ronaldo kick the ball to get that spin and dip on it from free-kicks. Fergie stood up in this little private jet with the ball, trying to show him how Ronaldo did it. James was seven or eight then and a massive Ronaldo fan, so he loved it.

Unlike Fergie at Old Trafford, I had less than three years to get it right at Liverpool and I definitely regret taking that job when I did. I think I would have been offered it at another, better time, if I hadn't accepted it then.

I took it on at the worst possible time. After the Hillsborough disaster, the players, understandably, were emotionally shot. They had gone to funerals for weeks. What that would do to me, God only knows, but I felt it left them traumatised.

Everybody told me not to take it when I did, but, as I have already explained, I felt suffocated by all the attention I was receiving in Scotland. At Rangers David Murray told me I would regret returning to Anfield, but there wasn't any football wisdom in him saying that, it was because of the healthy situation at Rangers. We had done the hard work. We had become the number one team and were a good bit ahead of Celtic, our biggest rivals.

Walter Smith was a large part of the reason why we had done a good job when I was there, but the foundations were well and truly laid for whoever got that job after me.

Walter originally agreed to join me at Anfield. I was with him and Phil Boersma in the sauna at the hotel across the road from Ibrox, when I told them I had been offered the Liverpool job and that I wanted them to come with me. For Phil, a former Liverpool player, it was like going back home, so he said yes immediately. Walter was also excited by it initially, but after some thought decided that going in beside Ronnie Moran and Roy Evans, who were always going to be part of my plans, wouldn't work out for him. He decided to stay at Rangers and I told David he should give Walter the manager's job. He was more than ready for it.

Peter, meanwhile, asked me, 'Do you really want this job? This is a job for a brave man.' Peter was as responsible as anybody for Liverpool's success over the years. He had been Shankly's man, Paisley's man, Fagan's man, Kenny's man and he said to me, 'Really, we only have one player', but after John Barnes, the player he was referring to, signed his new contract he got an Achilles injury, which are notoriously slow to heal.

I felt John allowed himself to get in his armchair after that. He went from the going rate at Liverpool then, which was about £200,000 a year, to £500,000, more than twice as much, and would have been easily the best-paid player in Britain at the time, I think he allowed himself to take his foot off the accelerator and I never saw the John Barnes that people spoke about.

Tom Saunders, another wise man at Anfield, who had also been there since Shankly's days, told me there was a major overhaul needed at the club, and I quickly realised that. Too many of the best players were the wrong side of 30. There were rumours that Kenny wanted to come back. I later wished he had.

Within six months I had Peter Beardsley wanting to leave. He was 30 and had a chance of going somewhere on his last lengthy contract. It turned out to be Everton. I had Steve McMahon say the same thing more or less. Ray Houghton told me his wife was homesick and wanted to go back to London. We agreed a deal with Chelsea, and he was going to see them that day, when I got a call from him.

'Ron Atkinson wants to talk to me, can I speak to him?'

'I thought you were homesick?' I said, and there was silence on the other end of the phone.

At that time, my attitude to it all was, 'If you want to leave, go.' I still thought of Liverpool as the place to be in European football. That was how I remembered the club. Obviously, these lads felt differently. I was too impetuous, though. I should have said, 'I hear you, allow me to get players in to replace you', because there was still a bit of life left in them.

Bruce Grobbelaar, Ronnie Whelan, Rushie, Steve Nicol and Jan Molby were all looking for testimonials. They were all main men at the club in their day and I think that emphasises what Tom and Peter said to me, that it was a team in need of a major refit.

The only criticism I have of Ronnie, Rushie and Steve is that they had allowed the dressing room to slip. I felt they supported me in every other respect. Their playing careers were on the wane, but I don't feel they let me down at all. Their personalities were not like an Alan Hansen or a Kenny Dalglish that would have kept dissenting voices at bay.

Robbie Fowler, Steve McManaman and Jamie Redknapp were at the other end of their careers. Robbie was 16 when I became manager, Steve had just turned 19 and Jamie was 18. These young boys went on to be really good players. Although they came in and did a job for me, you

FOOTBALL: MY LIFE, MY PASSION

always want to introduce kids into a team that's going really well, not one in transition. You don't want to damage them psychologically.

I saw worrying signs that standards had fallen since my playing days. One day against Wimbledon someone had defaced the famous 'This Is Anfield' sign, which appears as you go down the steps onto the pitch. They stuck a bit of paper on it with the word 'bothered' on it. I am told it was Vinnie Jones.

My players laughed and joked about it. None of them were angry about it and I was thinking what would have happened with previous teams. If someone had done that, we would have seen it as not just disrespectful to the current team but to everything that had been there before.

I know how the teams I played in would have reacted to that. They wouldn't have had a laugh and a joke about it. That was a cop-out and said everything about the dressing room I had. That fire that Liverpool always had was gone.

Peter asked me if I wanted to take over doing the players' contracts. I'd done that at Rangers and done well at it, in terms of buying and selling people. If people didn't work out, we turned them around and got them away pretty quickly. So I went into it with a lot of confidence, but, with hindsight, I shouldn't have been involved on the money side.

I signed Dean Saunders and within a week Ian Rush was at my door. He'd found out that Dean was getting slightly more money than him.

It was a period when transfers and salaries were going through the roof. I was saying to Ian on a Wednesday or a Thursday, 'Sorry, I can't give you any more money', and he was telling me what he'd done for the club. If I'd been him, I would have been the exact same. Then, on a Saturday, I was asking him to give me everything and more over 90 minutes. Getting involved in that side of things was a fundamental error on my part.

I signed four contracts in my seven seasons as a Liverpool player. Bob Paisley would simply say, 'There's a contract up there for you', and then you went to see Peter Robinson and there was no real negotiation. There was always a fair increase and Liverpool was where you wanted to be, there was nowhere else you wanted to go.

When I was player, the league changed from two points for a win to three, so as captain of the team I negotiated £125 per point with Peter. If we won, we were getting £375 extra. When I went back as manager, seven years later, and the money had gone through the roof, they were still on £125 per point. So the incentive to win hadn't increased, but the basic had enormously.

As a manager, you try to incentivise winning. The modern way is guaranteed money, whether you perform or not. That's not in anyone's interests in the long term. You are relying totally on the type of player you have. If you're earning £10,000 a week and someone offers you £375 to win a game, are you bothered?

I also had problems with criticism from a former playing colleague. I'd always got on very well with Tommy Smith. As a player, I would go out socially with him and he was Mr Liverpool. Everyone knew him. He was an abrasive character, but I liked him and enjoyed being in his company. I would stand and have a drink with him and we got on very well for the short period of time we overlapped as players.

When I went back as manager, he was still going into the boot room, but now he also had a column in the local paper and was being overcritical of the current players in it. From the dressing room, the players had to walk past the boot room in those days, and they could see him in there with his feet up on the skips for the kit, having a beer and laughing and joking. If I was a player walking past that, and he's inside the inner sanctum, I'd be thinking, 'They are condoning what he's writing about me', and it really was supercritical. So I had to say to Tommy, 'You can no longer go in the boot room', for that reason, and then he turned on me. I was merely sticking up for my players.

I made loads of mistakes. Letting Steve Staunton move to Aston Villa for £1.1 million just after I arrived was definitely one of them. With hindsight, my thinking was too heavily influenced by the stupid rule in force at the time that classed Irish, Scottish and Welsh players as foreigners. You weren't allowed more than three in your team for European games.

I also had David Burrows, who looked like he could become England's left-back at the time, and I thought he could only get better because he was in his early twenties. Steve was a very good player and turned out to be a great one, so letting him go was a big mistake, but it was partly forced on me.

Steve McMahon, Peter Beardsley and Ray Houghton were allowed to leave, not because they were no longer any good, but because they had told me they wanted to go, but I should have been stronger and resisted until I had replacements for them.

As for my signings, as I have said, I was into the same territory that Moyes and especially van Gaal were in recently at Manchester United. I was trying to buy replacements in a rush for established, older players and in that scenario you will make mistakes.

I feel very sorry now for Paul Stewart, given the knowledge about the abuse he suffered as a child. Back then when I signed him from Tottenham, I thought I was getting an aggressive, strong holding midfielder, but it just didn't happen for him at Liverpool. It didn't turn out the way I had planned, although now I can see that he had been through things that must have taken a terrible toll on him.

Most people thought that Nigel Clough was a good signing. He was similar to Kenny in many ways. A centre-forward but not an old-style centre-forward, what they call a false nine now: he was someone who I thought could link the play, chip in with goals and had a good football brain, but again he didn't fulfil the potential I saw in him.

I liked Mark Wright, but he would always drop off and defend, we couldn't get him to hold a high line. As a centre-half, he had the athleticism and size and was a good player. Neil 'Razor' Ruddock needed strong management, but I liked him, you knew when he went out he wanted to win and was prepared to noise up the opposition and his teammates.

I would also have liked to work with Julian Dicks longer. I thought he was a really good left-back. He came to us with a less than perfect knee, but I enjoyed working with him and thought he had outstanding quality. When I left they didn't fancy him at all, although that was maybe more to do with his personality than ability. Another signing of mine, David James, went on to be a very good goalkeeper. People point to him making mistakes, but all goalkeepers have their moments, nobody is perfect.

I missed out on two players, who went on to become legends at Manchester United. Peter Schmeichel wrote to me when I was at Liverpool in the early 1990s. Ron Yeats, the chief scout then, came into my office and told me there was a young Danish goalkeeper who was a Liverpool fan and was willing to pay his own travel and hotel in exchange for some time with us. But at the time I was trying to ease Bruce Grobbelaar out and that was proving a hassle, plus I had just signed David, so I thought I could do without a rookie keeper.

Eric Cantona was another I missed out on. We played Auxerre at home and Michel Platini came to see me afterwards. He said he had a player for me, a problem boy but a proper player. It was Cantona, but I said the last thing I needed was another problem player. I had 30-pluses that I was trying to get out, so I didn't need more hassle. I said I was looking for something else and so it was no thanks.

I was criticised for making too many changes but I was more than happy to work with Ronnie Moran and Roy Evans, which shows I respected the club's boot room traditions. I was still learning, and

Ronnie had worked with Bill Shankly, Bob Paisley and Joe Fagan, so I wanted to learn from him, and I got on really well with Roy. There was no problem with that dynamic.

The changes I did make were merely to make the club move with the times. Things like, 'Let's not get changed at Anfield anymore, let's go to Melwood and make that our base and put a restaurant there.' There was a real reluctance to do that.

The other thing I got greatly criticised for was doing away with the boot room, but when that story was flying around nobody mentioned that the club were pushed for space and the boot room had to go from one side of the corridor to the other.

It was like three steps away from where it used to be, but I was hung out to dry because I had 'done away' with the boot room. Peter and the board let me take the flak for that, when the reality was they were putting in a bigger media room where the boot room had been.

Other suggested changes by me were resisted. They used to have a really strong lager put on the team bus on a Friday in preparation for the return journey from an away game, and getting off the bus at Anfield after the game, nobody would have passed a breath test. So I simply asked, 'Can we put a weaker lager on there?' but there was always the same argument.

'We've always done it that way, we've won trophies doing it that way.'

'Any chance we can stop having fish and chips after a game?' I asked.

'We've always done that, too.'

When they talk now about the foreigners coming to England and improving our players in terms of their diet and less alcohol, that's what I tried to introduce in 1991, before any of them arrived. They were buying into it abroad and doing it for decades, but there was enormous resistance at Liverpool.

It was very easy for me to walk into Rangers and say to players, 'This is what we are going to do', because they hadn't won anything for such a long time and were obviously lesser players buying into it, thinking, 'This guy's done it and he's won stuff.'

Then I go to Liverpool and try and do the same things and they are not having it, because they have always won the big trophies while having the strong lager on the bus, getting absolutely hammered two or three times a week and eating fish and chips after a game. There was no appetite for change.

I should have quit after my heart operation in 1992 and the furore over my exclusive with the *Sun*. Instead I struggled on until January 1994, when I resigned after an FA Cup replay defeat to Bristol City at Anfield. I was in the Holiday Inn beforehand and could hear Russell Osman, their manager, give a scathing but accurate assessment of my side in his team talk through the wall.

'If we are aggressive and match them for effort, some of them don't like that and will roll over,' he said.

'You are spot on,' I thought.

Unlike Fergie at Old Trafford, I gave myself less than three years to get it right at Liverpool. Should I have stayed longer? I don't think so, because I had lost the support of some senior players and the board.

● ● ●

Managers are doomed with the culture of football now, especially the lack of patience from supporters at the big clubs – and both Liverpool and Manchester United are giants in football terms.

When you talk about football dynasties, it's impossible to stray very far from comparing things at Anfield and Old Trafford. Fergie got seven years before he won the league and four years before he won anything at all, but you are never going to get that anymore. With the phenomenal success they had under him, the current group of United supporters are used to turning up on a Saturday or Sunday afternoon and watching their team win and win well. All of a sudden, when Fergie stepped down, they were not doing that, so the bad feeling and negativity kicks in. 'You are not playing attractive football, you are not winning games, it's all down to the manager, let's get rid of him.'

It was difficult for me at Liverpool, but it was even more difficult for someone following Fergie because of how the game has moved on. There's less patience in the game now. It's all about today and instant success, and the fact that United have progressed into being one of the great, big financial institutions in world football doesn't actually help. They have put themselves into that top four with Real Madrid, Barcelona and Bayern Munich in terms of generating revenue and have to maintain that status.

With hindsight, maybe they should have gone for Jose Mourinho straight away. It was a job for someone with a personality that can deal with all the pressures that come with a big football club, but even Mourinho found it difficult in his first season because supporters are not willing to see it as a work in progress, not willing to see that a young player is going to be good in a few years' time. People want it in three weeks' time now.

When David Moyes stepped in after Fergie, his job at United, like mine at Liverpool, was to ease some legends of the club out the door, but when you do that at a big club, some of them don't want to go and they will make life difficult for you. He would have faced that, as players on the bench began to distance themselves from him when results didn't go their way.

At Liverpool, I had Ronnie and Roy, who I always got on really well with. Moyes had taken on former players as his backroom staff whose mates were still playing at United. That really is a vipers' nest, storing up problems, because they would have still been speaking to those ex-players, saying, 'This is not right, that's not right.' The relationships would have been more like between teammates rather than between players and coaching staff.

The dressing room dissidents would very quickly have worked out that Moyes was not going to be there too long. I don't believe he had that unflinching support you need from your players and that dynamic – where teammates over a long period of time at United, like Ryan Giggs and Phil Neville, were now on the bench as coaches – didn't help him either.

For a manager whose coat from the start is on a shoogly peg, as we say in Scotland, that's a very difficult situation to make work. He was never going to get the time to sort that out.

When I was managing, I thought the ideal was to buy someone at 22 or 23, who can come and do a job now, but can also only get better, then end up doubling in value. Yet experienced managers like Ron Atkinson, Harry Redknapp and Lawrie McMenemy would go out and buy the finished article, knowing there's not a lot of life left in them, but it gets you over that season. You are now looking at the next six to 10 games. That's how the game has evolved.

Fergie did that with Robin van Persie in his final season. He paid way over the odds, £24 million, for a 30-year-old, who, at Arsenal, had missed between a quarter and a third of most seasons through injury, but it turned out to be an inspired deal because he was the difference between United winning the league in that final season and not winning it.

Should Moyes have been given more time? Yes, in any sensible way of thinking about it, but the way our game has evolved, you simply don't get it anymore. It's about how good your lawyer is at negotiating the exit clause on your contract, because you know what's coming. We are never going to see anyone with the longevity of Fergie or Arsene Wenger again. Forget that.

So Louis van Gaal came in and looked at what Moyes did, how he kept his powder dry, which got him the sack within 12 months. The Dutchman's attitude was, 'I have to go out and immediately improve this lot', and had spent over £250 million on new players by the time he got fired.

Moyes attempted to go down the cautious, careful route, whereas van Gaal threw the kitchen sink at it. Every manager is a reaction to one that has gone before.

United, too, tried two different approaches to it from their perspective. First, on Fergie's recommendation, they went for Moyes at Everton, a super football club but not a giant. Then they went for van Gaal, who is used to managing mega-clubs like Barcelona and Bayern Munich, thinking, 'That's the perfect fit', and it didn't work either.

I don't think it would have made any difference whoever they got in first. They could have appointed Pep Guardiola, Mourinho or Wenger and it would have made no difference.

It's the expectation level that's the problem at United, and it was the same at Liverpool in my time as manager. If you have been the dominant force for 20 years, it's immediately, 'Why are we not dominating again?' There's no time to get your feet under the table. Whoever followed Fergie was doomed.

● ● ●

Am I amazed that Liverpool have still not won the league, 23 years after I left? No. Arsenal had a period where they had a really good team. United have had really good teams, then came Chelsea's period, then Manchester City's. It's the way the game has evolved.

We've talked about United being a financial giant. Arsenal had that period where French football has never thrown up such a strong group and Wenger had an insight before anyone else of what was happening there. Then you have Roman Abramovich's money coming into Chelsea, then the money coming into Manchester City, so I can't say I am amazed that Liverpool struggle to compete. I am saddened, like every other Liverpool supporter, but not surprised.

It didn't bother me in the slightest, though, when United surpassed Liverpool's record of 18 titles. I am still proud of contributing five to that total as a player. I would have loved to have added more as a manager.

United have got everything right off the field as well, which has turned them into this powerhouse that Peter Robinson had always warned about. Liverpool weren't a glamorous club compared to United, even back in their heyday.

Liverpool's population is also about a fifth of Manchester's. That came home to me when I was managing at Blackburn, how big a city Manchester was by comparison. There were four different ways I could go from south Manchester to Blackburn. Whichever way I went, the traffic would be rammed coming into Manchester. I didn't realise until then how big a city Manchester was, so Liverpool's 15 years of dominance was truly remarkable for a club and city of that size.

They are still the two biggest clubs in English football, the ones with the history. You can't buy that. When will Manchester City be regarded as a big club on the world stage? Not in my lifetime, I'd guess. It takes 20 to 30 years of non-stop success, of great players and great teams. There's also an affinity and affection because of the tragedies the clubs have been through. Hillsborough and Munich meant that there was a love and respect for the clubs from neutrals as well.

If you go to Old Trafford nice and early before a game, you see people walking round, taking in the history, taking pictures, wanting to be around the place. You get that at Anfield, too, but I am not sure you get it anywhere else to such a level.

Even on non-matchdays, you get people hanging around Anfield and Old Trafford. It's like going to Jerusalem, they just want to be there, almost as if it's a holy place.

What about the future for these two clubs? The jury is still out on Jose Mourinho and Jurgen Klopp, the latest two managers trying to re-establish those title-winning dynasties, in a game where the landscape has changed so dramatically.

MAN OF THE WORLD

I have already emphasised how great my childhood was. I went to live with my grandmother when I was 12, only because my grandfather had died and both my older brothers before me had done it for a few years between 12 and 15. It was never a conversation in our family, it was a duty.

The fact that I was living away from home before my teens helped me when I moved to London at the age of 15. My birthday is in May, and by June I was living in digs in north London. That hankering for new surroundings has followed me throughout my life since. I have lived in 27 houses now, from my childhood to living in digs to owning properties.

It irritates my wife greatly, but I could go home one night and suddenly say, 'I fancy going to live in Australia', and the only thing that would stop us is the kids basically. That's how I am and that's how I have always been.

There's a saying that a Scotsman will do anything for his country but live there. Maybe I fall into that category. Maybe I just have wanderlust. I have always thought the grass is greener on the other side of the hill. I've found out that's not the case on a few occasions, but I still look on these things as an adventure. I'm always excited by the unknown.

When I was 18 and on the Middlesbrough playing staff, for example, I got in a car with my pal Eric Carruthers in Edinburgh and said, 'Let's see how far we can get.' We ended up in Athens. We drove to the south coast, took the car ferry across to Calais and then headed south, through France, through Italy and through the country known then as Yugoslavia. We drove through what would now be the Balkans and several villages where it was all just horses and carts. There was nothing else. There were animals pulling ploughs in the fields. There were roads where you could look over the side into a ravine that if you fell into you would have died and never been found.

We were away for about a month and tried our best to drink those countries dry en route – beer, wine, whisky, brandy, the lot. Any fitness work was done on the dance floors of discos and we slept through an entire day at one point as we recovered from our revelry.

We caught the ferry from Piraeus in Greece to Brindisi, then drove up through Italy and then round the south of France to Lloret de Mar in Spain. I managed to literally drive into a wall in Spain and damaged the car's radiator, but we somehow managed to get it back to Edinburgh in the end. It was an adventure that left me with some fond memories, if not in great shape when I returned to Middlesbrough to find Jack Charlton waiting for me.

That spirit has never left me, though. When I went to play for Sampdoria in Italy in 1984, I was in my thirties, vastly experienced and had won everything. I was captain of the Liverpool team that had just won the European Cup, I was also captain of my country and my attitude was, 'Worst-case scenario, if it doesn't work out I can always come back.'

I had plenty of offers when I announced I was leaving Liverpool. I met Ken Bates, Chelsea's chairman then, in the Holiday Inn in Liverpool one night after we had played Newcastle in an FA Cup tie and he said, 'You can live in Guernsey and come over and do a couple of days' training a week.' I felt that if Italy didn't work out, doors would open elsewhere and so there was no fear about going abroad. Zero fear about the unknown in fact, and I come back to my personality as an explanation for that.

I fancied Italy and knew I could settle there. Nobody knows what the future holds for a player, so when I got offered, at 31, the chance to earn a great deal more money, plus all the best players in the world were in Italy at the time, I thought it was a no-brainer really.

Serie A was so popular in the 1980s. At Liverpool, we would have been the best-paid team in British football at the time and arguably Kenny Dalglish and I would have been the best-paid players. Yet before I kicked a ball for Sampdoria, I'd been paid more than I had netted in those seven years at Liverpool.

The same will apply, only multiplied by whatever number you like, for foreign lads coming to Britain today. This is the golden period for English football and the young men playing today must never forget that. They are getting paid astronomical amounts because TV is funding it and the public want to watch it. It's not because we have suddenly produced fabulous players.

Yes, I could have stayed at Liverpool and won more trophies, but I was ready for a change. I had spent my life being up for new challenges, something that excited me, but the big players here have no need to do that now.

Unless Barcelona, Real Madrid or, to a lesser extent, Bayern Munich want you, you don't go anywhere. Other than those three, if you are playing for a mid-table team in the Premier League, you are not going to get paid any more money elsewhere. There's no need to leave.

I don't see why anyone playing for Arsenal, Manchester United, Chelsea, Man City or Liverpool would want to move anywhere other than those three clubs I have mentioned. I don't think they need to.

A lot of the top players are here now, although the very best ones are still at the top two in Spain and Bayern Munich. I was playing against a different kind of player with a different mentality when I went to Italy, someone who saw the game differently. At Liverpool, I was playing with and against Englishmen, Scotsmen, Irishmen and Welshmen, by and large.

For some people, moving abroad broadens their horizons, but if the money wasn't so much better, would I have gone to challenge myself against the best players in the world, who were all collected in Italy at that point? Yes, that turned me on, having proved I could handle the English First Division and playing in Europe, and it was a new challenge to go and play against them every week, but I'm also honest enough to admit the icing on the cake was I would earn a lot more.

I signed a three-year deal to play in Italy and the original plan was to come back to Britain after that. If you were picking a world eleven at that time, they would almost all have been in Italy: Zico, Michel Platini, Zbigniew Boniek, Gaetano Scirea, Karl-Heinz Rummenigge, Michael Laudrup, Preben Elkjaer, Junior, Falcao, Cerezo, all the top men were there and Diego Maradona would later join Napoli from Barcelona.

At the end of my first season, there was a charity game arranged between an all-star Serie A select team and Verona, who, incredibly, had become Serie A champions that year. They had Elkjaer and Hans-Peter Briegel, the big German, as their two foreigners, so our scratch team turned up, we were all introduced to each other and then we won the game 6–0 in front of 60,000 people. We were just playing keep ball in the second half. So much for the theory that players need time to work together to understand each other.

Top players immediately pick up on each other's strengths. That day, I got an understanding of what the best in the world means compared to just very good players. I was standing behind Zico on two or three occasions. He's concentrating on the ball arriving and I'm seeing the picture, thinking, 'Go on then, there it is, out to the left', and he chooses to go to the right. The next time he receives it, I think, 'Through the middle', and he goes left. He was just able to see a different picture to what I could, and that really is what separates the greatest players from everybody else.

Sampdoria were a great club to play for and deal with, and I enjoyed my two seasons there. I had flown from Gatwick on the old British Caledonian airline to Genoa and when the plane rolled up on the tarmac, I emerged with my first wife, Peter Robinson and Liverpool's lawyer. There was no going through passport control. From the plane, we went straight into a car and straight into the city centre to Sampdoria's offices. I met Paolo Mantovani, the president, and we started to negotiate. There were three or four thousand people outside, blocking one of the main streets in Genoa.

The president had to go out onto the balcony and gesture to the supporters as if to say, 'Not yet, be patient', with his palms facing downwards. So I knew at that point I was in a great position to negotiate, although it was very easy with Mantovani, who was a gentleman. Austin Wilson, my then father-in-law, was a businessman and was going to negotiate for me. He was coming from Spain but flying into Rome and then being driven up from there.

He got involved in a traffic jam, so I ended up negotiating for myself.

We lived in Nervi on the Ligurian coast near Portofino in a big villa that had been converted into five apartments. I had the ground floor on one side and Trevor Francis, who had joined a couple of years before me, had the ground floor on the other. The back garden looked over the Mediterranean and ran down to it. It was just idyllic.

Nervi had one main street full of restaurants and cafes. It was a trendy, fashionable place, full of nice people. It couldn't have got any better. There was an international school for my two kids, Fraser and Chantelle, and Jordan was born while we were there. The children were all very young, but I think they benefited from the experience and still talk about it affectionately. It was all pluses on that score. I was lucky. I was living on the Italian Riviera.

Trevor and I became very good friends. We went to training and did everything socially together. As we lived next door to each other, whoever was first out in the morning would take four steps and knock on the other's front door. He was a very helpful and trustworthy friend, a thoroughly good guy, and Helen, his late wife, was great as well. Between the two of them they made that transition very easy for us as a family.

I later signed Trevor for Rangers, along with Mark Hateley and Ray Wilkins, who had both been at Milan before moving to France with Monaco and Paris Saint-Germain respectively. I knew their qualities. In Italy, they would change their foreign players regularly, not because they weren't doing well but just to excite the crowd, to give them a new or maybe a bigger name. There was nothing wrong with those players, as they proved when they came back to England. It was just the Italian way of stimulating interest from the fans.

When I left Liverpool, I did so with an open mind, but I quickly realised there was no easy way of playing football, there was no new way of training. They were not reinventing the game in Italy at that time. The training was different, but was it better? No. Nothing jumped out that made me change my game. If anything, I became less disciplined when I went to Italy. I abandoned the holding position I had occupied during my Liverpool days and went forward more.

It opened my eyes off the field, though. We have all been on summer holiday in a foreign country but to actually go and live there and see their approach to life is different. That was the biggest part of living abroad, the cultural change.

For example, at lunch, as we trained late afternoon in the summer, my new teammates all ordered a bottle of wine each. I thought, 'What's going on here, we're training in three hours' time', but the first thing they did was get the bottle, write their name on it, have a glass and hand it back. It was to last them for four or five days.

On a Saturday night, we would stay in a fabulous hotel in the middle of Genoa to prepare for our home game. We would be sitting as a team and the waiters would bring out a tray of steaks and cheese. In Britain, players would have wanted the steak and left the cheese, but in Italy they wanted the cheese with a bit of bread. I found that really strange.

I remember going to play Avellino in one game and they were all excited about going down to the south, as Avellino is inland from Naples, saying, 'Wait till you taste the coffee down there.' The water was supposed to be special or something. They ate their dinner so quickly that night and were all racing to get to the bar for a coffee. Another time, the bus was loaded up with wine because the guys all wanted a couple of cases to bring back.

The first summer I was there, we went down south to play a game and afterwards I said to Trevor Francis, 'I could murder a beer.' There was a little bar opened in the stadium and we took two mini bottles of beer with us onto the plane and drank them. I was hauled in front of the president the following day to be told we couldn't do that in Italy – it was all over two stubby, little bottles of beer.

The football too was interesting. Central midfielders generally get more of the ball than anybody else, have more touches, but playing in the pre-season friendlies with Sampdoria I wasn't getting as much of the ball as I would have liked or was accustomed to at Liverpool. I was thinking, 'Aye, aye, I'm going to have to work at this.'

Then, the minute the real stuff started, I got too much of it. After a couple of stray passes or a mistake, all of a sudden I was getting as much of the ball as I needed from my new teammates.

I played against all the great names I have already mentioned. While they had more success at international level than me, my CV with Liverpool, in terms of winning the league and European Cup on a regular basis, was a match for any of theirs.

I never felt, as you know by now, that they were better than me. I had no inferiority complex. I wanted to play against these players who some argued were the best in their positions and I enjoyed every minute of it. It turned me on.

I sometimes wonder what might have been if I had stayed longer with Sampdoria, because as a midfielder it was easier there than I was used to in England.

The Italian way was to drop off and let you have the ball until you were halfway inside their half; then they would come after you. In England, they were in your face on your own 18-yard line. It was different and I found it much more straightforward. I had a three-year contract that would have finished when I was 34, and I could have easily had another two years beyond that playing in Italy.

They used to change managers after six to 10 games and it was called the 'Italian disease' in Britain at the time. We'd say, 'How can they possibly do that', but look at us now. That's where we are now.

Is that because in Britain we have foreign owners, or because the public is demanding change, or maybe it's because no-one can contemplate dropping out of the Premier League? The FA Cup now means so little, because it's all about the Premier League, all about the money. You cannot afford to be out of it or, if you are in the Championship, it's all about getting into the Premier League because that is the only way your club can grow.

We had success at Sampdoria, too, winning the Coppa Italia in my first season and laying the foundation of the side that would go on

Left: **My first day at Rangers, July 1986, with David Holmes and Freddie Fletcher. In David Holmes and David Murray, I had two chairmen who supported me to the hilt.**

Above: Walter Smith was the most important signing I made in my time at Rangers.

Above: Bringing Terry Butcher to Ibrox was crucial. He was the England captain at the time. His arrival made it easier to attract other players from down south and elsewhere.

Left: July 1989. Signing Mo Johnston was done for the right reasons: he was a fine footballer.

Below: With David Murray in January 1990. It was a very special time in my life.

Above: Being unveiled as the Liverpool manager in front of the media, April 1991.

Left: Ronnie Moran was the biggest influence in my career.

Below: About to lead my first training session at Melwood.

Above: Striding out at Anfield before my first match as Liverpool manager.

Left: May 1992. Embraced by Ronnie Moran after our FA Cup final victory against Sunderland. I had come out of hospital, after a month, just the day before.

Below: The passion of the Galatasaray fans is truly unique. Here they are honouring my flag-planting episode when I was manager there.

Left: I enjoyed my short time at Southampton. Due to circumstances, I felt I had to resign after just a year there. I wish my stay had been longer.

Below: I was given just six games as manager of Torino – that's almost par for the course now in the Premier League.

Left: Benfica are a truly great football club on the world stage. Managing them was a fantastic experience. I loved it there.

Above: March 2000. Managing Blackburn was one of the most enjoyable jobs I had, working for good people. I regret leaving. I should have stayed longer.

Above: May 2001. Celebrating promotion to the Premier League.

Right: February 2002. Lifting the Worthington Cup trophy after beating Spurs in Cardiff.

Above: I was appointed manager of Newcastle United in September 2004, and it was arguably my most difficult job. It is a club which deserves to be doing well in the Premier League, but a succession of top managers have failed to deliver a trophy for the fans.

Above: With Craig Bellamy (left) and Kieron Dyer (right). It was an interesting time to be managing a unique club.

Getting my fix of football with Sky Sports, without the pressures of playing or managing.

to win Serie A in 1991 and reach the European Cup final a year later. I was brought in because I was a senior player and they had a young team – Gianluca Vialli was 20, Roberto Mancini 19 – that just needed a bit of guidance as it grew up.

● ● ●

My next adventure abroad was as a manager and came on the back of me resigning at Liverpool and having had open-heart surgery. So, of course, I chose somewhere peaceful and relaxing for my next job – managing Galatasaray in Istanbul.

I'd had other offers after Liverpool, but none of them got me excited. I was enjoying my year off, pottering away in the garden of my new house. Then I got the call to ask if I would be interested in joining Galatasaray.

I'd read about the fanaticism of their supporters, but I'd never been to Istanbul. I got a call from a guy called Denny Caouki, whose brother was on the board of Galatasaray and who became one of my dearest friends, and I met him in Paris along with a couple of the directors. They were smart businessmen, who had a passion for their football club. They reminded me of Rangers and Celtic supporters back in Scotland, in that you do not become a fan of those clubs, you are born one.

I went out to Istanbul and there were thousands of fans at the airport to greet me when I arrived. I went to see their final league game. After 15 minutes, they were 3–0 down at home, yet ended up still winning. It excited me, but I was venturing into the unknown. I knew nothing about Turkish football, nothing about Turkey, but the people I'd met had convinced me within five minutes that I would love it out there and that's how it turned out.

It was one of the best times of my managerial career. I enjoyed living there and my daughter went to the international school there. We loved Istanbul, made some great friends and the football went well.

Fenerbahce were our main rivals. They always seemed to have an edge on us. They had Carlos Parreira, the former Brazil manager, in charge but we beat them in the cup final and, of course, then came the famous incident with me and the flag in the centre circle afterwards.

When I first joined, a Fenerbahce director had done a piece in the paper saying: 'What are Galatasaray doing signing a cripple?' He was quite a mouthy guy, whose picture appeared in the papers quite regularly, so I came to know his face only too well. Nine months later, we won the first game of the two-leg cup final 1–0 in our stadium. In the second leg, we were losing 1–0 in their stadium, an extremely hostile environment, when the ball dropped to Dean Saunders in the final minute of extra-time. Dean and I of course go back to my time as Liverpool manager, and so I knew what he could offer in Turkey. He's a wonderful striker of a ball, so the moment it left his foot I was off my seat, knowing it would go in.

We went down onto the pitch after the game to celebrate. Our players went down to where our supporters were. I jogged down there and a huge Galatasaray flag on a pole was handed over the wire fence to us. The players all took it in turns to wave it. I took my turn and they all ran up to the halfway line to get the cup. As I followed them up to the halfway line, I looked up to the emptying stands, and could see this Fenerbahce guy who I recognised in the directors' box. It was a moment of madness on my part, of thinking, 'I'll show you who is a cripple', so I went to the centre circle and planted the flag there.

I quickly realised that the Fenerbahce fans were not terribly thrilled with my actions. I made it to the tunnel, although I had to duck under the plastic shields of the police to do so unscathed. I was just thinking, 'I've got away with that', when I was confronted by a Fenerbahce supporter who had got into the tunnel, so I ended up having a bit of a stramash with him.

I got into dressing room and thought, 'Well, that's it, I will be on the first plane out of here tomorrow, they'll sack me for sure', but when the Galatasaray directors came down, they had tears in their eyes and I have never kissed and hugged as many moustachioed men in my life. I was sitting in the dressing room with my right hand in an ice bucket because I'd punched the guy who attacked me, thinking, 'This is strange.' I had armed guards at my home for a while after-wards. It was just one of those things that happened.

The flag planting was not me trying to demean Fenerbahce, it was me making a point to a guy who had been extremely rude and disrespectful to me when I arrived in Turkey. If you go into the

Galatasaray offices in the city centre now, behind the reception desk there's a life-sized picture of me planting the flag, and when they play at home now they sweep the stadium beforehand to make sure no supporter tries to get on and do the same thing.

There's a machismo about things like that in Turkey, which is a bit like Scotland and the Old Firm in many ways. You get the same sort of stuff. Who's bigger in Scotland, Rangers or Celtic? In Turkey, is it Galatasaray or Fenerbahce? Galatasaray see themselves as the aristocrats of the football world out there, and I have to say they justified that with the way they dealt with me. Everything they said, they kept their word.

I'd signed a one-year contract because the board were in the last year of their three-year term, so they said they could only offer me a year, but if they were re-elected they would offer me another couple. They didn't get re-elected, but my contract said if they didn't notify me by a certain date they had to pay me another year's wages.

Well, the date came and went and when I pointed this out to them after they lost the election, it was a very simple deal to do. We came to an arrangement that they were happy with and I was happy with. I didn't play hardball, which I could have easily done, and that was out of respect for the guys I worked with at the football club.

That's the one job I look back on and think life could have been very different, because whoever got that job at that time was taking over a young team that was going to dominate Turkish football for six or seven years. That's exactly what they did, because they had the nucleus of the team that won the Uefa Cup in 2000 and the Turkey side that finished third at the 2002 World Cup in Japan and South Korea. As their manager, you were destined to have success.

If I had signed for another two years, then I might still be living in Turkey now, that's how much I enjoyed it. Istanbul was an exciting place and I only have nice things to say about it. It's the one job that might have tempted me back into management.

The best two players in my time there were Tugay Kerimoglu and Hakan Sukur. They were both fabulous for me. Hakan got married in a big celebrity-style wedding that was televised live in Turkey. It was at the Polat Renaissance hotel in Istanbul, round the swimming pool, the most magnificent setting. Halfway through the proceedings, Fethullah Gulen, the famous Turkish preacher, turned up and it was like Jesus Christ appearing at a wedding in our country. People had tears in their eyes just being in his company.

After football, Hakan became an MP and he was critical of Recep Erdogan and the government. Gulen and Erdogan, now the Turkish president but back then the mayor of Istanbul, were once friendly but they have since had a major falling out and Gulen has had to go into exile, as has Hakan.

Hakan's first marriage was short-lived and I can remember not understanding exactly what the supporters were shouting at him at away games, but getting the general idea. In Turkey, when a woman leaves the house it's a real criticism of the man and he had to dig deep because he's an emotional fellow, Hakan, an absolute gentleman.

He and Tugay did the business for me. Tugay was a cheeky chappy, but those two in their prime would have got in any team.

The British players I signed for Galatasaray had mixed fortunes there. Barry Venison didn't last very long and neither did Mike Marsh. Both of them found life difficult there. Barry was an experienced player, a holding midfielder. The way he trained was always intense, with his Liverpool background, and he upset the Turkish players and it became a bit of a kicking match in the five-a-sides.

Mike's wife found it difficult and he went back early, too. Mike would side with Barry in training and that was the last thing I needed. I couldn't have that, because as I was speaking in English the Turkish lads were thinking, 'Is he siding with them?', so it became a bit of an impossible situation.

Then I got Brad Friedel and Dean Saunders in and with their personalities they were warmly accepted and both were great for me out there. Dean was one of my regrets at Liverpool, he scored 23 goals in one year there, but I had other players, big-name players at the club, telling me they couldn't play with him, so I stupidly let him go and he went to Villa.

I got Dean back at Galatasaray and wherever I've had him after that, either as a coach or a player, he's been outstanding for me on and off the pitch. If I was going back to football management tomorrow, the first person I would ring would be Dean to ask him to be my assistant again. He's knowledgeable and he's got a personality which works well in the dressing room.

It could be a bit lively at times in Istanbul and not only when I was planting a flag in the centre circle of our main rivals' pitch. There was something of a gun culture there, which could be alarming. We would train on Saturdays before Sunday games. I'd have dinner with the players afterwards and because I had a young family then and lived in the centre of Istanbul, to be close to the international school, and the training ground was in an area called Florya, which was an hour's drive away, I'd head back to see Karen and the kids.

The players would go off to their beds and I would leave Ahmet, my assistant, in charge. He was Turkish but had been brought up in Germany and spoke English perfectly, plus several other languages. He was a real disciplinarian who took no nonsense, a good football man. A Turkish version, if you like, of Walter Smith, my assistant at Rangers.

Ahmet was an enormous help to me, because it's really important when someone is translating for you that he gets the correct message across. I'd leave him in charge on a Saturday night and leave the training camp, maybe around 7.30 to 8pm after we had eaten together and the players had gone to their beds, then I would come back in the morning.

After one particular night, I came back in the morning and Ahmet was waiting for me as I pulled into the training ground. 'We have a big problem,' he said. Then he told me what happened. The players went to the games room, put some pillows and cushions at one end, got their guns out and created a shooting gallery 30 metres long with a target in front of the cushions and fired live rounds at it for their Saturday night entertainment. Even in Istanbul, I had to discipline them for that.

After the last league game of the season, where Fenerbahce won the championship, we had beaten Besiktas in their stadium, which sits right next to the Bosphorus, so we had to drive alongside it on the way back to Florya towards the airport. All the Fenerbahce fans were out on the street, tooting their horns and the traffic came to a standstill.

I was at the front of the bus and Dean Saunders was at the back, and the Fenerbahce supporters soon worked out it was our bus and were out of their cars, banging on the window. This guy started banging on the back window and Arif Erdem, who was our centre-forward, a good player who got a goal at Old Trafford when Galatasaray knocked Manchester United out the European Cup a couple of years before, went into his bag, got his gun out and pointed it at these guys banging on the window and they sensibly scattered. Welcome to Istanbul.

Everybody from home asked me if it was anything like *Midnight Express*, the film prison drama which did not paint a flattering picture of Turkey. I replied, 'Absolutely not.' Although when I first arrived, there was an incident with Adnan Polat, the vice-president, who was taking me into town for a very nice lunch with my wife and afterwards to look at some houses. We were in traffic. A car pulled up, four or five cars in front of us, and a guy jumped out with a gun in his hand and started chasing another fella up a street. Who knows what was going on, but I think there must have been a bit of road rage, Turkish style.

● ● ●

My time at Torino, my next foreign staging post, was too brief for such stories, or for me to have the same fondness that I still have for Galatasaray. I'd resigned from Southampton and met these Torino representatives at an Italian restaurant in Knightsbridge, took a punt and went out to Italy and they said, 'You'll be really excited, we have signed 18 new players for you, our friends in the press and among the agents recommended them to us, they are all top players.' One of them was Gianluigi Lentini, who had returned to the club having been a world transfer record going from Torino to Milan for £13 million in 1992, but then was involved in a very serious car crash. He got badly bashed up and had some head injuries and was never the same in his second spell at the club.

They gave me six games and I drew two, lost two and won two. Looking back, my Italian wasn't good enough. In Turkey, I could get away with a translator, but really in Italy you were expected to speak to the press and that was something I hadn't taken on board. It made it doubly difficult.

That was also the first time I'd experienced the sports science people creeping into football. Today, every club has a sports science department and they appear to control a lot of stuff that managers normally would be in charge of. They come out with things like the optimum time to put a substitute on is 68 minutes, or this player looks tired and his stats are down, rest him this week. They have far too big a say in football matters now.

These guys cannot stand on a touchline and watch a small-sided game and say, 'He's worked his socks off in that game . . . this one's going through the motions . . . that player could do more.' They are relying on stats-based information all the time. They can put a monitor on most of the muscles on your body and on the biggest one, your heart, but what they cannot do is monitor what goes on inside your head. Everybody has a different threshold. Some people feel exhausted and can go again. Others give up.

At Torino, they were known as the *professori*. The players all used to wear these monitors and there would be days every week where they had to do their 600-yard runs, their eight 75-yard sprints, their ten 50-yard sprints.

I'd say to them, 'Let's have a small game', and they would look at each other as if to say, 'But we have not done our work yet.' I wanted them to play in the games and get a feel of the ball and every single time I was overruled.

You were very much the coach, it was clear the sports scientists would deal with the fitness of the players and you would just decide what tactics to use. Having learnt from the likes of Fagan, Paisley and Stein, I found the sports science people taking the lead tough to accept.

There were signs that some of the players were beginning to grasp what I was after, but you need more than six games. They were decent people and they paid me what I was due. Torino was a yo-yo club then between Serie A and Serie B, living in the shadow of Juventus, who are the most successful club in the history of Italian football. We used to play at Stadio delle Alpi, a stadium built on the outskirts of Turin for the 1990 World Cup, and we had 20,000 supporters in a 67,000-capacity arena. It had zero atmosphere and we didn't have a proper training ground either.

After four months in Italy, I was preparing to move on again.

● ● ●

I was offered a chance to go to Benfica, a deal in which Steve Archibald, my former Scotland teammate, was involved. Joao Vale e Azevedo was in the middle of his election campaign and needed a famous manager as part of it. I went to one of his rallies, it was like a US presidential one, he was then elected and I agreed to go out there, all within two weeks of leaving Torino.

I quickly realised Benfica were the Rangers, Celtic or Manchester United of Portugal, with an enormous support and equally inflated expectation level. They were seventh when I went there and we ended up in second place in my first season.

Dean Saunders turned up on my doorstep again and did a great job for me. I brought in Michael Thomas as a holding midfielder, he couldn't do anything flash, I thought he got the job done, but they didn't take to him. Then I took Brian Deane there and Mark Pembridge, who, again, was a really solid midfielder. They all came for little or no money in terms of transfer fees. The Latins have that extra flair, but I wanted something more solid and reliable. Thomas and Pembridge gave me that, but didn't have a trick, so they weren't deemed to be good players in Portugal. In fact they were bloody good players.

I worked out before too long that it was a difficult job. I'd come in some mornings and the players would be sitting around demoralised and I'd ask the team liaison officer, who was an ex-Benfica player from Mozambique and Eusebio's mate, what was wrong. He would say, 'They have not been paid again', so I phoned Azevedo and said, 'I've got a problem, the players are feeling low, I am going to get nothing from them this week, unless they get paid.' He'd reply, 'But I had the liaison officer in here yesterday and gave him the cheques, I don't understand what's happening.' I'd put the phone down and say, 'He says you were in his office yesterday and he physically gave you the cheques himself.' The liaison man would reply, 'I've not been to that office for months.'

It became embarrassing at times when we didn't pay for players we had signed. Karel Poborsky, who we owed Manchester United £2 million for, was an example. I was getting calls from back in Britain to ask if Azevedo was going to pay the money. I had no idea at that point that he had no money, no idea that he was taking money from the club. In the end, I just couldn't make any calls to anyone to sign players. It was all just smoke and mirrors.

Azevedo has since spent several years in jail for fraud. He was telling me stuff, knowing that within 30 seconds of me putting the phone down on him that I was going to find out it wasn't true. I had to go through Uefa to get my compensation afterwards and didn't get everything I was due, which was disappointing. I'd signed an initial two-year contract, then I got another two years but at the end of the second year I was sacked.

Before that, Ray Clarke, who had started off at Tottenham with me and remained a pal, phoned to recommend a striker we should sign. Ray had played in Holland for Ajax for a couple of years and was scouting there. He told me, 'There's a centre-forward playing for Heerenveen that you should come and have a look at.'

I went to Holland and was extremely impressed and persuaded the president we should buy this player and he should have a look himself to see why. We got on a plane at Lisbon airport, a KLM flight that was going Lisbon–Porto–Amsterdam. On the morning of the flight, Ray said we should check the weather because the game we were going to see might not be on due to fog in Holland. We checked at the airport in Lisbon and it was still on. We got to Porto and I went to the doors of the plane to get a phone signal and Ray said, 'The game's been called off.' So we got off the plane and had to drive back down to Lisbon. The striker Benfica missed out on? Ruud van Nistelrooy.

I admit now that I took all these jobs without doing my homework properly. It was a privilege to work for such a great club as Benfica, with its history and the passion people have for it. It's up there with Galatasaray, Rangers and Liverpool in that respect. Portugal is my favourite holiday destination, they are extremely pro-British, and I love going back there. I love the food and people and I can see myself spending my retirement years there.

As roguish as Azevedo was, and despite the difficulties I had with him at Benfica, I actually liked him. We were never going to become champions of Portugal. We would get close to Porto, the dominant club, but there was always the feeling we weren't getting a fair deal from certain referees when we were up north, where the power base of Portuguese football is, not Lisbon. Benfica were never going to win the Portuguese league in those days.

I don't know if it was just the way it translated, but in Portugal they talked about winning a new contract with a good season. Some of the players would get in their armchairs after that.

I had a young player called Hugo Leal. He was 17 and got in the team and right away his agent is knocking on the door because he's had good reviews. He later went to play for Atletico Madrid and Paris Saint-Germain. He was like Brian Laudrup, that sort of dribbler type, with enormous potential. He played a couple of games, received the plaudits, then his agent was in there, demanding a new contract.

The president gave him a new contract. Then a white BMW appeared in the garage each morning – a fast one. I remember driving home from an away game, going down the motorway and I saw some of the players standing by the side of the road, with this BMW rammed into the safety barrier.

The president was under pressure to give Leal a new contract after a couple of games. The world of football has become like that now. We talk about a player being great, when they're not. He's had half a good season, but that word great is used far too easily.

People said about the player, 'He's world-class.' No, he's not. Define a world-class player? Could he play for Barcelona or Real Madrid? Could he play for Bayern Munich, Juventus or PSG? No, he couldn't, so then he's not one of the best in his position in the world.

That story from my time at Benfica, about giving somebody too much too soon, increasingly applies to our football. We spoil players and they end up with an attitude problem because everybody out there on the street respects them, not for what they have achieved in the game, but for the lifestyle that football has given them and the money that football has given them. They are treated with a respect they are not due, given a title that they have not earned and that makes them a different animal from the players of my generation, who probably deserved more money and respect than many of them received.

Although I loved my adventures abroad, both as a player and a manager, I didn't want everything I saw during them to follow me back to Britain.

THE LION TAMER

When I was offered the Newcastle job in September 2004, my first thought was, 'I will be the one to turn this club around. I will be the one to prod this sleeping giant awake.'

I was like every other person who is offered that job: I wanted to win Newcastle United a trophy, their first major one since the old Fairs Cup in 1969 or, domestically, the FA Cup in 1955. It was a huge challenge, of course, but my thinking was, 'I've won lots of trophies elsewhere, I can do it here as well.'

Taking over from the late Sir Bobby Robson, a local hero with whom the Newcastle supporters clearly identified, was a bit like succeeding Kenny Dalglish at Liverpool. Through the years, I had not made life easy for myself in that respect. I had not taken the easiest choices in terms of the clubs I managed and the people I had to follow, but I had never felt any of that was going to be a problem to me.

I vividly remember the very first time I went to Newcastle. I was in an executive box with Sir John Hall and Freddy Shepherd, the directors, when Freddy's wife turned to me and said, 'So you're the Lion Tamer, are you?' There was a feeling at the club that under Sir Bobby the young bucks in the squad had been able to run wild, walking off from training and just being generally disruptive. So they needed their new man to get things under control.

I believed back then, and still believe now, that there's got to be a boss in whatever business you are in, and that's how I saw football management. The strong characters in that Newcastle squad – the likes of Lee Bowyer, Kieron Dyer and Craig Bellamy – had to do it my way.

Bellamy was difficult, for sure, but I got him in terms of the fact that he wanted to be a better player. It was the first time I'd heard a player tell me, 'I'm ready to go to the next level, what can you do to help me get there?' He was a frustrating boy to work with at times, but there was also a lot to like about him. He had ability and was a bit like Jamie Vardy at Leicester City now, in the way he played up front.

Part of the problem was that the Newcastle players were put on such a pedestal in the city, more so than a lot of other places. For players who hadn't won anything, they were treated like royalty by the supporters. Wherever they went, they were held in such high regard. Newcastle is a bit of an outpost in the north of England compared to the rest of the Premier League, and the supporters worship the players who move there as a result of that.

They particularly love a centre-forward, a goalscorer, and they love a character as well. My problem was these types needed to fit into a team ethic and some of those boys were, without any criticism of Bobby Robson, allowed to get away with things which I wasn't prepared to put up with. I would never tolerate people walking out of training if they felt it wasn't right. I would certainly never tolerate someone feigning injury, which I did experience with Bellamy at Newcastle.

Craig didn't want to play in the wider areas, he felt he was a through-the-middle man and then he feigned injury before a game against Arsenal in January 2005, which was very disappointing and led to him leaving the club. I wanted him to play wide in that game, but he wanted to play as a central striker.

As I came out for a training session before the game, he was walking off past me, so I asked him what was wrong. He said he was feeling tightness in his calf or hamstring. Later, when I saw Dean Saunders, my assistant, he said the senior players had told him that Craig had told them he was going to feign an injury. I confronted Craig and took him to see Freddy Shepherd, and in the end he admitted he was feigning injury. It was impossible after that for us to work together in my opinion, so he was shipped out on loan to Celtic.

We hadn't hit it off from the start, it's fair to say. The previous

October, not long after I had taken charge, he swore at me after being substituted in a 1–1 draw at Charlton, which was Sky's Super Sunday game that weekend. The dressing rooms were down near one corner and the dugout was near the halfway line, and he's looked up towards me and called me an 'effing prick' as he came off and the cameras and microphones caught him doing so.

I hadn't noticed it myself, but at the end of game Dean told me, 'He's mouthed off at you.'

'Not a problem,' I replied.

At our next team meeting, the boys asked if I was going to say anything to Bellamy.

'No.'

Lo and behold, he was sitting in the front row in this meeting and, as I was talking, he kept shaking his head.

'What is it that you are not agreeing with?' I said, and before he could answer me, I added, 'Can we just go back over the last seven days of your life. You have told John Toshack he's not getting the best from you with Wales, because he's not using you in the correct position. You have told our chairman that St James' Park doesn't suit Craig Bellamy and then on Saturday you called me an effing prick.'

That's when I physically got hold of him and I asked him to come into the gym with me. I walked out of that meeting and thought, 'What am I doing? Is this job for me?' It was a pivotal moment in my management career, perhaps the beginning of the end of it for me. I thought, 'Do I really need this? Is this what it has come to?'

Alan Shearer was good for me, and supportive, apart from refusing to stop speaking to a local journalist who was constantly critical, but Bellamy and him used to be at each other all the time, too. It was mostly banter, but sometimes went beyond that. I think there was a genuine dislike between them there.

There wasn't the same animosity between Lee Bowyer and Kieron Dyer, although you wouldn't have known that when they went for each other on the pitch during a 3–0 defeat at home to Aston Villa. Their infamous fight came after a really good run of 12 matches unbeaten in all competitions through February and March, which had carried us to the FA Cup semi-finals and the quarter-finals of the Uefa Cup, but our season fell apart after it.

My recollection is you could just feel the tension and the frustration building in the stadium that day. Bowyer felt he should have received a pass from Dyer that he didn't get, and then the two of them were having words, having forgotten the game was still taking place. They were shouting at each other, and they started to walk towards each other. I came off the bench and I was screaming, 'No!', because I could see they had completely lost it. Then the two of them traded a few blows and were both sent off.

I took them into the press conference with me afterwards and asked them to explain themselves. I had them beside me and said to the assembled media, 'Here they are, if you have any questions, ask them and they can answer them for you.' They apologised for their actions, although not to each other.

It was a difficult job, probably the most difficult I encountered in my management career, including Liverpool. I made a mistake when Alan Shearer was going to chuck it in by persuading him to play on and give me another year because I felt he was good in the dressing room. In doing so, we only ended up getting Michael Owen in during the summer, when, in reality, we needed two strikers. Alan was on his last legs and if he hadn't stayed on, I think we would have ended up getting the two we needed.

Initially, I'd wanted to sign Nicolas Anelka. I'd had a meeting with his brother, who also acted as his agent, in my house in Cheshire, and I'd also spoken to the sporting director at Fenerbahce and they were willing to sell him. The player wanted to come, too, but Freddy Shepherd wanted Michael Owen instead, so we got Owen for £17 million from Real Madrid, but only after his preferred return to Liverpool had fallen through.

Michael had spent the day at Freddy's house near Morpeth. There were pictures of him there, so the press had clearly been tipped off. Then he left and was going to give us his answer. This was just before the transfer deadline, so we arranged to meet at St James' Park. I was there along with Freddy Shepherd, Sir John Hall's son, Douglas, Dean Saunders, and Paul Stretford, the football agent who worked with Freddy's son, Kenny.

Michael was going to phone them, but the call never came and they started to panic. It had got to about half-past ten at night and I was about to leave when they suddenly said, 'Before you go, have a look at these.' Paul Stretford came in with a pile of CVs and said, 'What about one of these?'

He handed me about 50 pages of players who were top scorers in all the leagues in Europe. 'Pick one of them,' he said. Unbelievable. Less than 48 hours before the transfer deadline, I was being asked to pick a player who I'd never seen play, because he had a track record of scoring goals and because they thought they were not getting Michael.

I just said, 'I'm going home.' Dean Saunders lived opposite me and at about one in the morning, he was throwing stones at my window to wake me up – I'd turned my mobile off by this point – to tell me Michael Owen had phoned and said he was coming to Newcastle United after all. You couldn't make it up.

This was typical of the club. I'd watch a game at night, come in and have breakfast with my staff at the training ground and I would say a throwaway line like, 'Did you see the game last night, such and such played really well.' That was all I said, but on three or four occasions Kenny Shepherd would come back to me and say, 'We've spoken to his agent, he'd love to join us.'

I'd only said he had a good game, not that I wanted him or thought he would fit in. That's how Newcastle was run, so what chance have you got?

There was work to be done in getting other players in. We paid Rangers £8 million for Jean-Alain Boumsong in a bid to sort out the defence, but it didn't work out as I hoped it would. Of course he could have done better, but we never really had a solid partner for him. Titus Bramble and Boumsong were perhaps too similar. I then signed Craig Moore from Rangers to be a steady Eddie beside Boumsong, because what we had were two centre-halves who were a bit hit and miss.

I felt with the right partner beside him, Boumsong would show what he was capable of. He was athletic and went on to play for Juventus and his country. There was a player in there, but he didn't show his true capability at Newcastle.

The club also asked about Albert Luque, a Spanish winger, after we had played Deportivo La Coruna in a pre-season friendly. I said he was worth signing if we could get him in for £2–3 million, but we ended up paying £9 million for him.

Around 20,000 fans turned up for Michael Owen's unveiling, another example of the club's incredible support, and things were going pretty well until the final minute of the first half at Tottenham on 31 December 2005. Michael was smashed by Paul Robinson, their goalkeeper, in a one-on-one, and stayed down as the half-time whistle went. I turned to Dean and said, 'If he's out for any period of time, we might as well hand our resignations in now.' Those were prophetic words on my part.

Tottenham actually have an X-ray machine at White Hart Lane, so about 15 minutes into the second half, the doc came out, stood in front of me and said, 'Bad news, Michael has broken a metatarsal.' I knew there and then that the clock was ticking on us, because without him we weren't going to score any goals.

That's how it played out. Shortly afterwards, we lost 3–1 away to Manchester City and the club's player liaison officer came to the training ground with a letter. I could see he knew what was in it. I was sacked by letter. It wasn't face to face, which didn't surprise me at all.

Newcastle was the job that made me realise that management was no longer for me. I found managing the players difficult and working for the board doubly so. I remember saying to Glenn Hoddle when someone was sacked at West Ham, 'That would be a good job for you', and he said he didn't fancy working with Karren Brady there. I said, 'Glenn, there's a Karren Brady at every football club now, and they think they know more than you and me put together.'

Everyone gets the same treatment at Newcastle. The support can be fantastic when things are going well, but the frustration born out of not winning a trophy since 1969 soon surfaces when the going gets tough. They see clubs like Blackburn or Birmingham winning something, or Leicester winning the Premier League, and they say, 'Why can't that be us?' I think they need to let someone have a real run at it, someone they believe in. Maybe they have found that manager in Rafa Benitez now.

There's almost an argument for them staying in the Championship, when they are winning games there and everyone is happy. Time and time again, the supporters there have had their hopes built up and it has ended in failure and disappointment for them. You have to be winning games there. If you're not, you are only two away from a full-on crisis.

Of all the managerial jobs I had, even when you factor in my time at Benfica, Galatasaray, Liverpool and Rangers, being Newcastle boss was the most difficult one. That was where you were under the most pressure, where you felt your head was constantly in the noose.

Mrs Shepherd was right when she said, 'So you're the Lion Tamer, are you?'

● ● ●

With hindsight, I should never have left what I had at Blackburn for the madhouse at Newcastle. I definitely regret doing so. I had four of my happiest years in management at Blackburn and it was a mistake to leave. If I hadn't left Blackburn then, I would probably still be in management now. My time at Newcastle soured my experience of it and put me off doing it again.

I had tremendous support from John Williams, Blackburn's chief executive. He would come down to the training ground every lunch-time, or certainly three or four times a week, to talk over any concerns he had. It would drive me mad sometimes, but I knew it always would come from the heart and I was cool about that. If he had anything to say, he would say it to my face.

At most clubs, it isn't like that. I enjoyed working with John, with Tom Finn, the secretary, and Robert Coar, the chairman. That's not always the case at a football club and certainly wasn't at Newcastle. At that time, Blackburn were a very well-run club.

I was living in Hampshire and spending a lot of time on my garden, when the call came from John to ask if I would be interested in going there. Yes, I would, I replied. I arranged to meet them at a hotel next to the M6 in the Midlands and I was excited by it immediately.

At the time, Jack Walker was still alive. They had been relegated with Brian Kidd as manager and John was keen for me to hit the ground running for the next season, so I went in there in March 2000 and signed an initial two-year deal and it was a great working environment.

I remember Manchester City coming to Ewood Park and winning promotion and thinking, 'I don't want that happening again, I want it to be us celebrating out there.' You don't want other teams celebrating on your pitch. It was a case of assessing the squad and then the aim was to push for promotion the year afterwards.

Even when we didn't have a great start to that season no-one panicked, everyone stuck together. It was a case of, what can we do better, not, what can my teammates do better. I always had faith that with the characters and the quality of player we had, we would be good enough to go up.

We had Alan Kelly and John Filan as two very good goalkeepers, before we brought Brad Friedel in, and we had Garry Flitcroft and Craig Short, who were proper professionals. They were vital because you spend so little time with players that you need your senior pros to be big characters. Garry was an absolute warrior and a great captain, and Craig Short was a no-nonsense centre-back. They were both throwbacks to an earlier era in a sense.

We also had some really exciting younger players. I had Damien Duff on one wing, Matt Jansen was on fire up front and David Dunn, who had such fabulous ability, was in midfield. I inherited a good squad of players.

John felt we were playing too much football, but I told him to stay calm because football would always win the day. I quickly got immersed in it, because the people from that area are really solid. It was almost old-school English football: a great board of directors, local businessmen who were in it for all the right reasons, with Jack Walker in the background as benefactor.

I met Jack when I was manager of Liverpool, but never when I was boss at Blackburn, where it quickly became obvious that he was seriously ill, because he never came to any games. The fact that he wasn't making the trip over from his home in Jersey was a bad sign, and sure enough he passed away less than six months after I joined. It was still a good club, run on the principles he had put in place, but after his death the spending power of Blackburn was greatly reduced.

The Championship was a difficult league, but I always felt we were good enough to go up in my first full season. As a manager, it's a good feeling to know that, and also to know that there is that togetherness. We only lost three games from mid-October to the end of the season. We beat Burnley in the derby at Turf Moor and then 5–0 at Ewood Park, while a 4–1 win at Bolton proved the key to clinching the second automatic promotion place behind Jean Tigana's Fulham, something we finally achieved with a win at Preston in our penultimate match.

Most clubs who go up target survival, but I felt we were good enough to aim higher than that back in the Premier League. I had some money to spend and arguably my best purchase with it was paying £1.3 million to Rangers for Tugay, who I knew from Galatasaray.

He had a great sense of humour and knew more English than he let on sometimes. Tugay's passing game in the middle of the field was a big part of our style of play. He had great technique and was a fantastic distributor of the ball. I just wish I had been able to bring him to England earlier in his career, because he would have been an even better player then. I've worked with some magically skilful players – John Barnes, Matt Le Tissier, Davie Cooper at Rangers – but I would have to put Tugay up there with them.

We finished 10th in our first season back in the Premier League, but the campaign is best remembered for winning the League Cup in Cardiff. On the way there, we beat Arsenal 4–0 in the quarter-final and then Tottenham 2–1 in the final.

Glenn Hoddle was manager of Tottenham and they were the fancied team. We had signed Yordi, a Spanish centre-forward, on the recommendation of Michael Robinson, my former Liverpool teammate. He turned out to be a bit of a throwback and did really well for us in his six months at the club. He came on in the final as a substitute for us in one of his first games.

Garry Flitcroft couldn't play, he was suspended, so I put Mark Hughes in midfield and he terrorised Tottenham. Matt Jansen put us ahead, Christian Ziege equalised, then Andy Cole scored the winner in the second half and Brad Friedel made a couple of good saves to see us through.

I still look upon that win as an excellent achievement. There are only three major trophies you can win in England at the start of each season and that's one of them. For Blackburn at that time, with their spending power relative to the bigger clubs, it was punching above their weight. There was a good team spirit and we had a really solid outfit, with strong characters like Henning Berg, Brad Friedel and Craig Short. With players like that in the dressing room, you don't hear about the problems.

That's the way a football club should be. These players were taking responsibility. It wasn't, 'I'll just train and then go home in my Bentley to my big house and take my wages.' These lads cared about the dressing room and saw it as their responsibility to get involved in issues and sort them out if they felt they weren't right. They were prepared to put their heads above the parapet and, as I've said before, that's what is missing today from the big players at many clubs.

Building on that League Cup win wasn't easy but we managed it, finishing sixth the following season, 2002–03. To get promoted at the first time of asking, to win a major trophy, to finish sixth and to qualify for Europe twice – I still consider that a successful time.

I would have liked to have done more in Europe, but we lost to Celtic in the year they went on to the Uefa Cup final. We should have won the first leg at their place in front of 60,000 people. Unfortunately, Henrik Larsson got a goal early on at Ewood and from then on the momentum was with them.

The year after, we played the Turkish side Genclerbirligi and I was really disappointed to lose that. We were beaten 3–1 in the first leg, but we could have scored 10 in the second game at Ewood.

Then the bank started to put some pressure on the club to sell players. Damien Duff joined Chelsea for £17 million and David Dunn was sold to Birmingham for £5.5 million.

Damien was very special as a young man and had a very good career. In many ways, he was too honest because he wanted to do everything. He wanted to be closing down when we didn't have the ball, he wanted to be sprinting back 30 or 40 yards to get into position and he wanted to be doing the damage going forward. He used to get hamstring injuries because he put such a shift in. It was a case of trying to get him to be tactically better, where he didn't have to be sprinting back all the time to get in position, but he was a delight to work with.

David Dunn should have had a similar career to Duff's, but it didn't work out that way for him. I remember having a conversation with Dunny and asking him, 'What type of player do you want to be?' He saw himself as a sort of Paul Gascoigne, dribbling from midfield and getting into the box and scoring goals, but I always felt his shape was going to be against him doing that, and that he could be a really good holding player in midfield because he had great feet and was strong. I don't believe David Dunn ever reached the heights he should have. I wish now that I'd worked with him longer.

The same was true for Matt Jansen, but that was down to the poor boy's misfortune more than anything else. Phil Batty, the club doctor, would hand the players a list of what they could and couldn't do in the summer at the end of each season. There was no water skiing or horse riding. It was a case of don't go on a donkey on Blackpool beach, never mind a horse.

There were also no motorbikes, but Matt was on holiday with his wife in Rome when the moped they were on was hit by a taxi at a crossroads. He was in a coma for six days, suffered a head injury and his football career was never the same after that.

I was not easy on Andy Cole and Dwight Yorke, because I was determined they wouldn't let their standards drop at Blackburn after being at Manchester United. I had a confrontation with Dwight after putting in a heavy challenge on him in a training game, which I regret. I shouldn't have been trying to play five-a-side at 50 years of age.

I still work with them both on occasion on television now and we speak about our relationship back then. I would not have been their favourite person. I felt they had come from United thinking, 'We did this and that there', and allowed themselves to get in their armchairs a bit. That was in my head to begin with, and I was always hard on them because of it.

I don't think they particularly enjoyed their time at Blackburn, but they were two very special players and they had a responsibility to turn up every day and be proper professionals around those who weren't as good as them. That's how I saw it anyway. They were two top men in their field and they should have been keen to pass on good habits to the lesser ones.

It couldn't be a case of Dwight and Andy picking and choosing when they wanted to train properly, because if the people who don't have the ability go down that road, then they are never going to give you anything. The lesser lights have to be bang at it every day and you are looking for your top men to show that, but at least we can have a laugh and a chuckle about it now when we look back.

I was also hard on Keith Gillespie, another former Manchester United man. He will look back on his career and think he could have done so much more. He was rapid and brave, great qualities to have, but he had the same haunted look as George Best. He would wish he could do it all again now, because he had the potential to play for a long time at United or one of the other big clubs. He definitely had the attributes to do that, but there's no way you can be fully concentrated on your football if you are losing serious money gambling as he was.

We finished 15th in my fourth season, although I never felt we would be relegated. My last game before I left was at home to

Manchester United. We were winning 1–0, then in added time Louis Saha used his hand to divert the ball to teammate Alan Smith and they scored. After the game, I was asked if I was interested in the Newcastle job.

I think at the time John Williams was fairly happy about the deal, because they were getting good compensation for me and Mark Hughes would be inheriting a team with some decent players. The fans at Blackburn were very fair to me, they weren't on your back straight away, they gave you time and got behind you.

● ● ●

The supporters at Southampton were similar in my season there from 1996 to 1997, in that they also had sensible expectations of their team. At The Dell they were getting gates of 15,000, and at that time a far higher percentage of a club's income was generated through gate receipts. Attendances at that level would not allow you to buy the sorts of players teams like Southampton, Hull and Bournemouth can go and buy today, because gate money now is small beer compared to television money and where you finish in the league. It's just a fraction, unless you have 75,000-strong crowds every week like Manchester United.

I liked Southampton as a club and loved the area so much that I still live there now. I went there after Galatasaray because Barry Venison had made the same move and recommended me to Lawrie McMenemy, their director of football. I met Lawrie and got on very well with him from day one and signed a three-year deal. They managed to keep it quiet; I stayed at Lawrie's house the night before it was announced, then went to their training ground in Hampshire and was wowed by it. I told him, 'You should have brought me here first, that would have made negotiations easier.'

Initially, it was an old-school board of directors. A local accountant was the chairman, Guy Askham. They were all nice people and assured me they were going to be there for the three years that I signed for. Unfortunately, within six months they had brought on board a guy called Rupert Lowe and, within a short space of time, I realised I couldn't work with him.

As far as I could tell, he knew absolutely nothing about football, but was soon telling us all where we were going wrong. He would ask stupid questions like, 'Are they fit enough?', although he really meant Matt Le Tissier rather than the rest of the squad. 'I've a friend who is a lecturer at Loughborough College who could help with that,' he added. 'Is Le Tissier the right choice as captain?'

I immediately said to Lawrie, 'I'm going to struggle with this guy.' They had just avoided relegation, but we brought in a couple of good Norwegian players – Egil Ostenstad, who started scoring immediately after signing, and Claus Lundekvam, who spent over a decade at the club. We also signed little Eyal Berkovic on loan as a creative midfielder and he did well, too.

The highlight of that season was beating Manchester United 6–3 at The Dell. Roy Keane was sent off early on and we ran riot, Ostenstad scoring a hat-trick, but I remember saying afterwards that United would still win the league and they proved me right. We finished 16th, a point above the relegation places.

It was nip and tuck right to the end. After the season finished, Lawrie and I were going to watch a game in Norway to look at Tore Andre Flo, who eventually signed for Chelsea, and I remember saying to him on our way back to a board meeting that unless Rupert Lowe came up with a decent budget to get a few more players in, then I wasn't going to stay. He ended up offering me a transfer budget of £2 million and I decided that I couldn't keep Southampton up on that.

They wouldn't have survived so long in the Premier League if it hadn't been for Matt Le Tissier, as talented a footballer as I played with or worked with at any club. He was Mr Southampton. He wanted to be fitter, but whenever we pushed him he would break down, tearing a few fibres in a thigh or a calf muscle, so in the end we decided to leave him as he was. He still single-handedly kept Southampton in the Premier League year after year.

He was an incredible talent and a really nice fellow. He must have realised his importance to that group of players, but he never acted in a difficult way or as a Billy big-time. He had a great sense of humour and good banter with everyone.

The thing that was so attractive about his personality, that easy-going, laid-back Channel Islander charm, was probably what stopped him going to a bigger club. Money was not the driver for Matt. He enjoyed playing football the way he wanted to play. If he wanted to have a go in training, he would have a go. If he wanted an easy day, we would leave him because on a Saturday he would always turn up for the team.

Any kid reading this book, who wants to go and have a look at great goals being scored, should go and have a look at some of Matt's spectacular goals. What would he be worth today, playing in that role just off the front, with no responsibilities for getting the ball back, just doing damage going forward? He would be priceless today on these perfect pitches, I reckon.

We were always asking a bit more of him, but you just accepted that when the games were tight he would make the difference. With penalties, you might as well have just given us a goal because he never missed them, and he was fantastic with corners and free-kicks as well.

Yet it was a player who came on as substitute for Matt in a defeat to Leeds United at The Dell in November 1996 for which my season at Southampton is still often remembered. Ali Dia was just one of several trialists we were taking a punt on at that stage, because our squad was so small. Some worked out and some, like Dia, certainly didn't.

We initially got little Berkovic on a similar deal, for example. We went to Scotland for pre-season and couldn't register him, so we had him play in a friendly at Dunfermline and used a youth team player's name, which was a bit naughty, but we got away with it.

Someone then received a call saying George Weah had a cousin in England who wanted to come in on trial. We were a small team on the south coast and were taking players in on a regular basis because we had no budget to work with, so we got him in for a week's trial.

After the first 10 minutes of the first training session, we knew this guy Ali Dia was not good enough, but decided to let him stay for the rest of the week out of kindness. We were going to say to him on the Thursday or the Friday, 'Thanks, but no thanks.'

As the week went on, we got injury after injury and we were down to the bare bones, so we had to name him as a substitute. Terry Cooper said to me, 'We're going to have to include that fool in the group for Saturday.' I initially said no, but I was persuaded to do it because we had nobody else. He was only registered for a month, because that was the minimum you could register someone for.

We were playing Leeds at home when Matt had to come off after half an hour. Having a look along the bench, we only had centre-halves and full-backs on it apart from Dia – he was the only forward, so we threw him on. He had a marvellous talent for arriving where the ball had just been rather than where it actually was, so we took him off again before the end.

The story doing the rounds was that we were all conned, we were all fools. The reality is we knew exactly, after 10 minutes of the first training session, that he wasn't very good, but circumstances dictated that he got a chance when he shouldn't have.

I thought I could put him on and he would run forward without the ball and be a nuisance, but he couldn't even do that for us. I had serious football people like Terry Cooper, Phil Boersma and Alan Murray with me at Southampton and nobody was being conned or tricked for a second. It was necessity that led to Dia's infamous appearance.

I was only sacked three times as a manager, by Benfica, Torino and Newcastle. I left Liverpool by mutual agreement. I left Rangers and Blackburn for other jobs, although I probably shouldn't have on both occasions. I only signed a year's contract at Galatasaray, and I resigned from Southampton after a year there.

Overall, my managerial record stands up to scrutiny. I won four league titles with Rangers and four League Cups, plus domestic cups for Liverpool, Galatasaray and Blackburn. It doesn't quite compare to my playing career in terms of silverware, yet is still a decent return.

I don't miss being a football manager at all, but I am proud of my record as one.

MANAGEMENT
MADNESS

I feel much better since I got out of football management. There's still a part of me that misses it – watching a game I sometimes find myself thinking, 'If I was in there, I would do this and that', but then reality bites.

You look at the results on a Saturday night and you think about the teams and players that are having a good Saturday night and a good weekend, and the others who will be lower than a snake's belly, and that's until they play another game of football.

Ultimately, for me, the good times were not outweighing the bad. The high I was feeling when we won a game, didn't compensate for that feeling of loneliness, and, I know it might sound dramatic, the despair, when we lost. It just left you feeling so responsible to your employers and your supporters. I couldn't close my office door, walk away from the training ground and leave it there.

I took it home with me and was a very different person there. I'd be quiet, I wouldn't be noisy and having arguments, because you are constantly thinking of what else you could have done. When I was managing, it was 24/7.

That might seem a throwaway line, but if I was anywhere at any time and there was a lull in the conversation, I would start to drift off and think about the issues I had in the football world. I just couldn't leave it alone and I think most managers are the same. If there's anyone out there who's different, they are very lucky.

I never put myself up for any job after leaving Newcastle in 2006. Why did I pack it in? That last job cheesed me off to the point where I wanted out completely. I'd never been at a club before where it was every man for himself to such an extent. No-one cared about anyone else. There was no togetherness. The job is hard enough when everyone is pulling in the same direction.

I didn't want to put myself in that situation anymore, where I would be answerable to the people that own and control football clubs. At every single club now, you have a chief executive, director or chairman that knows more than you.

What used to happen, going back a bit, is that football agents befriended managers because they wanted you to do deals with them. Then the agents quickly worked out that managers come and go and might not be around in six months' time. So they started to befriend the director of football instead, the chief executive and ultimately, if they could, the owners and the decision-makers, because they were going to be there a lot longer than the managers.

Whichever way you look at it, the tail wags the dog in football now. You fall out with one player, who might be worth £10 million, but his mate might be worth £20 million, and his mate might be worth £25 million, and so on. You end up falling out with four or five at least. Then you have a couple of indifferent results and their agents are on the phone to the chief executive, the directors, the owner, the chairman, saying, 'Do you know he's lost the dressing room?'

That's the beginning of the slippery slope for the manager, the beginning of the end. You are undermined from every side. Only Fergie, certainly, and maybe Arsene Wenger, were above that situation; every other manager was vulnerable to it.

The best two examples of player power undermining managers in recent seasons are Jose Mourinho at Chelsea and Claudio Ranieri at Leicester, both disgracefully sacked the season after winning the Premier League. That's the power of the modern player. If you fall out with a couple of them, you are toast.

If you sign five players and two of them don't work out, the board stop valuing your opinion and start to pay attention to the opinion of others. Look at the West Ham situation, where you have Jack Sullivan, son of the owner David Sullivan, on social media criticising the manager's selections, substitutions and signings. All of that is unacceptable.

Directors of football are fine if they are in place before the manager and part of the process of hiring him. I had Lawrie McMenemy as one at Southampton and that worked very well because Lawrie respected me and I respected him. He was vastly experienced, so I valued his opinion. He knew how the politics of football worked and how Southampton worked at that time.

Most importantly, I took the job knowing that was the situation. The problem arises if you take a job where there's no director of football, and after a few indifferent or bad results, it's then put to you that they should get a director of football in to help you out.

It doesn't matter how they couch the suggestion or proposal, it's basically saying, 'We don't think you are doing that good a job.' Then that person becomes the voice that the directors, owners or chief executive listen to. If you walk into a club and there's one in place and you are told up front that you are going to be working with someone, you accept it. If it's put to you after you have been in the position for a period of time, that's when it gets difficult.

● ● ●

I should have appreciated more the autonomy I had at Rangers to get on with the job without any interference. One ritual I had there was to have my blood pressure checked before matches. It was that horrible time when you have spoken to the lads, they have gone out to warm up and there's nothing else you can do.

I used to confide in Donald Cruickshank, the doctor at Rangers then, who was a wise old owl. I enjoyed those five to 10 minutes, because he always talked so much sense and it stopped me thinking about what was going to happen in the match. He always told me my blood pressure was a little high, but still normal. You would expect that before a game, wouldn't you?

Yet, after nine months back at Liverpool, that started to change. My blood pressure increased and was now classed as very high.

I used to eat dinner quite late. There was an Italian in Knutsford just off the M6 and I'd go there and maybe grab a bite at 10 at night and then down a couple of espressos afterwards. One night, during the time when I'd bought a house and was having some work done to it, I was living in a granny flat area and I remember not being able to get to sleep because my heart was racing. I put it down to the coffee, but later ended up in hospital undergoing tests.

I was asked to take an electrocardiogram and then a second one under stress. It revealed that I'd suffered a mild heart attack.

Next was an angiogram after which I was told I needed a triple heart-bypass operation. My cardiologist at the time said that there are two types of people. He told me I was Type A, where if I'd had a nine-to-five job, got home at half past five, with my dinner on the table and settled down to watch television at six as my routine, Monday to Friday, that would have been stressful for me with my personality. Then there is Type B, who would have found doing what I'd been doing extremely stressful and wouldn't be able to cope.

There was definitely an element of that in my life, but my major problem was genetic. I had two uncles who died prematurely, one in his thirties and the other in his forties. My dad had a triple heart-bypass when he was 70, so it was always going to be an issue for me at some stage.

When I was working, I constantly had the feeling of someone poking me in the breast with their index finger quite hard. I lived with that and I would be rolling my shoulder subconsciously. Within a couple of weeks of stopping work that disappeared, so stress definitely contributes to mental illness or physical illness, without a shadow of doubt.

I was diagnosed late on the Thursday morning. After they told me I needed a triple heart-bypass I immediately said, 'When can you do it?' The consultant went away and came back half an hour later and said they could do it on the Tuesday.

That was also the weekend of Liverpool's FA Cup semi-final against Portsmouth, but I simply said, 'Let's do it.' It was something I had to deal with and I wanted to confront it there and then.

The night before the operation a nurse came into my room, told me to get out of bed and stand on the chair naked, and then ran a felt-tip pen down the veins on the inside of my leg. I was completely shaved from the armpits down, by this time, and not a pretty sight. This was all in case they needed to use any of those veins during the operation. It was the moment I knew this was for real.

The Norwegian surgeon then came in about 9pm and said, 'You

will be going down at 7am, you will be down there for four or five hours.' Basically, he just went through the whole process. So I said to him, 'Make sure you go home and have an early night now', and he said, 'No, I'm off to the pub', and then he starts telling me about this pub round the corner from the hospital where they sold real ale.

He said he went there for a couple of pints, two or three times a week. I said, 'Make sure it's only two pints', and went to bed with that in my head.

The following morning was just the normal routine of preparing me for the op. Into theatre and, as the anaesthetist got to work, I settled into a peaceful state. I quite enjoy being knocked out. I like the feeling of drifting off, that three or four seconds where you know what's happening before you're out for the count and the surgeons are doing their thing.

None of that was a big deal for me. I'd witnessed my dad going through it. I was determined to be the best patient they had ever had. I remember soon after the operation they had me up walking, I was on a bike and then I had this infection. The scariest period for me was when they opened me up again. I had a lovely neat scar from the first operation, because there's obviously stitching involved when they cut your sternum. All that had to be re-done. The infection had to be treated.

I remember being back in the intensive care unit, with just a night-light on, and no-one else around, thinking to myself, 'This is how you die, so I'm not going to sleep.' I just kept looking at the clock. That was the only the time I was frightened in the entire process.

When I got this infection, I also had fluid on the lung. They basically didn't know what was happening, but I was suffocating. I can remember being in the room and telling them, 'You have to do something, I can't breathe.' There must have been four or five doctors looking at each other and Karen was leaning against the wall and so distressed to see the state I was in that she fainted.

In the end, this guy took the initiative, rolled me on my side and stuck something into me three times, so they could drain my lungs. I still have the equivalent of three stab wounds on the left side of my chest. I have never experienced anything as painful as when the fluid was leaving my lungs, but it did the desired trick and I was able to breathe again. My mother had died of emphysema, so I had witnessed someone who couldn't breathe and how distressing it was, and I had similar symptoms.

Following the blood pressure medication, which knocked me down a few levels, I was feeling vulnerable for the very first time in my life. All of a sudden, you are looking at yourself when you are cleaning your teeth or combing your hair and your eyes drop down to your chest and you have a huge scar there now. Post-operation, it's not a particularly attractive sight. I prided myself into my late twenties on how I had very few scars on me, then all of a sudden I am covered in scars, from taking a vein out of my leg to the one on my chest. Previously, I was feeling invincible, as though I could deal with anything;

then you realise you are just like everybody else and have weaknesses like everyone else.

That's when the comfort blanket of having a really solid family foundation came into play. Thinking of my parents and two older brothers, I realised that's where my confidence and self-belief came from, and that helped me get through that traumatic period in my life.

Post-operation, I drifted in and out of having the right attitude to football. I couldn't leave it or turn it off, at first. I should have resigned as Liverpool manager immediately after my operation, but my attitude then was still, 'I am only going to be in this hospital for 10 days and within a couple of months I will be myself again.' Well, it didn't work out like that.

I ended up being in hospital for 28 days once I'd developed the infection, and in that month things went pear-shaped, with the *Sun* publishing a picture of me after the operation, on the day of the Hillsborough anniversary. It would have appeared the previous day if our semi-final against Portsmouth hadn't gone to extra-time and penalties, but it was still my fault for agreeing to it and an exclusive article, which appeared two days before.

I had been working in Scotland at the time of Hillsborough in 1989 and seriously misjudged the depth of feeling on Merseyside. I should have resigned there and then. It ultimately soured my relationship with the Liverpool supporters forever and it's something I deeply regret. If I could turn one thing round in my football career, it would be that.

I've been to the Hillsborough services a few times. I think that the supporters respect that I know I made a mistake. Nobody comes up and confronts me, but I get that a lot of them will never accept my reasons for doing the *Sun* article, or the circumstances of how it ended up appearing on the anniversary.

It didn't take me a couple of months to recover from surgery, it took the best part of a year for me to become myself again. Nobody warned me about the psychological effect, which I am not ashamed to talk about now. I found myself becoming tearful and very emotional at the slightest of things.

When I was in the hospital and the press were still parked outside, I'd sneak out the back for a walk in the woods and one day I ended up taking a shortcut through them and came to a fence and suddenly thought, 'If I fall over here and they don't find me . . .' I had a panic attack because I had come off the path and nobody warned me about that. That vulnerability was completely foreign to me.

Another time, after a 4–2 defeat at Aston Villa, best remembered now for Ronny Rosenthal missing a sitter for Liverpool, I had arranged to go out for dinner with Ron Atkinson and our wives, but after the game, I just said, 'I can't go out tonight.' I had tears in my eyes all the way home on the M6. With all those warning signs, I should have chucked it in.

I certainly shouldn't have gone to the 1992 FA Cup final against Sunderland. I just felt it was important I was there. I wanted to judge the reaction of the supporters to the *Sun* article, and the vast majority were okay with me. I expected it to be hostile, but they were more than fair with me.

I should have read the signs that the club had distanced themselves from me because of the *Sun* story. I came out of hospital and had to make my own way to the airport and then my own way from Heathrow to the team hotel at St Albans before the Cup final. There was no car waiting for me or anything.

I should have stepped down after we won the FA Cup. Instead I carried on, which, when I look back now, was madness on my part, particularly as I had seen one of my own managers effectively die in the dugout.

Jock Stein collapsed towards the end of Scotland's tense World Cup qualifying draw with Wales on 10 September 1985. I was suspended for the game, which we drew 1–1 thanks to Davie Cooper's penalty nine minutes from the end, and saw the tragedy unfold at first hand.

Jock was 62, roughly the same age as I am now, when he died, so I can relate to what happened to him that night. His story would have been similar to mine: a mixture of bad genes and doing the wrong job for too long and then, at 62, being in a situation where you are carrying the weight and expectation of the nation on your shoulders. It was that fatal cocktail of factors which ultimately cost him his life.

They say Scots have a terrible propensity for heart problems. People say things like, 'Look at the size of him, he's overweight, he's at risk of having a heart attack', but that's not the only factor. You can have overweight people who have great cholesterol levels and the skinny guy who has terrible cholesterol. The more stress you have though, the more of the bad chemicals you produce that also increase your risk.

I remember at half-time we were under pressure, 1–0 down to a Mark Hughes goal. There was me, Fergie and Jock, and he was asking us what he should do. It wasn't like Jock to turn to other people for advice. With hindsight, that was maybe a sign he wasn't right.

After Davie's penalty, the photographers were literally in his face, he was struggling to see what was happening on the pitch. It was such an important moment and photographers push their luck, don't they? They are worried about someone else getting a shot that they don't get, but it all added to the pressure on Jock that night.

I was standing in the corridor at the top of the tunnel and I saw Jock, after he had collapsed in the dugout, being taken into the treatment room. It had swing doors on it, like those old Western saloon doors, so every time people came rushing out I could see him on the bed, slanted to one side with the oxygen mask on and the late Stewart Hillis, the Scotland doctor, working on him, trying to resuscitate him. Big Jock never regained consciousness.

● ● ●

I was 38 when I had my life-saving heart operation. Looking back now, I was way too intense. I was used to getting my own way on the pitch when I played, and then I became a manager and used to get my own way most of the time at Rangers, too. We were winning nearly every week. Of course, there were disappointments throughout my playing career and in management, but it was mostly more of the same – winning.

Then I moved to England, to a far more difficult job. I don't make an apology for it, but I hated the feeling that losing gave me. I just didn't enjoy that and I would maybe rant and rave too much when that happened. Looking back, I was too hard on certain individuals, who weren't capable of dealing with the kind of pressure I was trying to put them under, and my demands were too great.

If I had my time again, I would be very different. I would be more appreciative of people's feelings. More appreciative that not everyone can be that focused and that determined. We are all different. I would just be a more understanding human being I think.

There's no major stress in my life now. I have the same worries everyone else has. I have kids and you wonder what will become of them. You want to see them all settled, that's my main worry and focus really. What I do now in the TV studio I don't find stressful in the slightest. I enjoy it.

It's about finding a balance that someone of my vintage can feel relaxed about. Psychologically, being able to pick and choose what you want to do is very good for you. You don't have to be somewhere at a certain time, you don't have to be doing so many games, you can decide how many. I am lucky in that respect. I don't really have any pressures now, other than the ones that most people have.

I've always been a good sleeper, with the help of a glass of red wine. Another thing which has helped me enormously in terms of keeping sane, if I have issues in terms of calls I don't want to make or mail I don't want to answer, is going to the gym and getting the endorphins flying around the body. I come out of there feeling revitalised. When I was managing I used to go before a game on a Saturday or a Sunday to the gym and it helped me cool my nerves, and put me in a better place psychologically.

I don't think any manager deals with the stress of the job well. Perhaps the best I encountered was Ron Atkinson. After Villa had beaten us one Saturday and I couldn't face going out for dinner, he said, 'Come on, it's only a game.' I thought, 'You have never witnessed how I am at home when we are on a bad run.'

Ron's personality was as good as anyone's, though. He managed Manchester United when things weren't always going well, but he was laughing and joking through that as much as anyone I can think of.

You look at Alex Ferguson and in front of the cameras he was two different people before and after a game. I remember watching him on the touchline at Wembley in 2011 when Manchester United lost 3–1 to Barcelona in the Champions League final. The camera focused in on him, then panned down to his hands and he was visibly shaking.

Tell me if that's okay for a 69-year-old man, as he was then. How can that be good for you? He was in a real state.

The ones with any longevity still struggle with the stress of the job, like Arsene Wenger, in 2016, pushing a fourth official and getting banned from the touchline for four matches. Someone of that experience, who comes across as so calm and calculating, after more than 20 years at Arsenal, doing that? Then you have Alan Pardew head-butting David Meyler, the Hull player, in 2014, when he was managing Newcastle. It makes you, in some cases, not a nice person to be around.

At Rangers, although it turned into a great number for me, there was pressure early on, but I was young and up for any sort of challenge flung at me back then. The responsibility of trying to re-establish Liverpool was different, more stressful.

You often look back at things you would have done differently and I shouldn't have left Blackburn for Newcastle either. I worked for good people there. The crowd weren't dreamers. If they were in the Premier League now, they would be dancing down the street. They had realistic aims.

At Blackburn we won the League Cup in 2002, then finished sixth the following season and the board of directors were good. I mainly worked with John Williams, the chief executive. As I alluded to earlier, he was a pain in the backside but at the same time fabulous to work with.

John kept me on my toes. There wasn't a week where we didn't have a noisy argument, but it would be forgotten there and then by both of us. It was onwards and upwards, then he would be down the next day and we would be arguing about something else. I responded to that. I liked working with him because he cared. He was in charge of Jack Walker's money and felt a responsibility for it. I liked that about him.

Since leaving Newcastle in 2006, I've not been tempted back into club management. I went to an interview for the Scotland job at the Hilton hotel at Edinburgh airport before George Burley succeeded Alex McLeish in 2008. I met Gordon Smith, then SFA chief executive, Campbell Ogilvie, who I knew from Rangers, and George Peat, then president of the SFA.

They asked me what I'd require and I told them it would be more than they paid my predecessor. I thought it went well, but I never heard anything else and then I read in the papers they had given it to George. They never even had the courtesy to give me a call.

I also turned down a lucrative offer to return to Turkey with Trabzonspor, and over the years since I have been asked by agents if they could throw my hat into the ring for jobs. My answer was always the same. No.

● ● ●

I would say, because of the interest in football today, the scrutiny is greater and more widespread than ever before. The single biggest driver for that was the conversion of stadiums into refurbished, all-seater venues in the 1990s. You could go to stadiums before that and not find a ladies' toilet. They slowly began making it attractive to women and their daughters, whereas before it used to be a dads and lads sport. I get recognised by women as much as men now. That's a new phenomenon from when I was a player.

The profile of the players and managers is enormous now. Previously, it was only the top dozen players in the country who would get recognised. Now Joe Average can be a household name in some cases. With that comes an enormous responsibility because people recognise you, and it's how you handle yourself in public that's important. Some of these young lads find that a problem.

For managers that only compounds the pressure. You can't go anywhere without being recognised because you are on the telly all the time, so I would say there is more stress now. It's not like if you work in another industry and you are having a bad time, a bad day or a bad week, you can walk around and nobody knows that, outside of your immediate family or colleagues.

For a football manager, on a Saturday or a Sunday, the world knows you have had a bad day and the world knows you are getting criticised, so it's doubly difficult. It has never been tougher on a manager than it is now.

Social media is not something I get involved in. I have no interest in it, but I am sure it makes it even harder for managers. I am lucky that I don't need anybody to tell me if I have had a bad day, so I don't look at social media. I don't understand it and I don't understand why footballers use it. It's dark territory to me, but it would be another pressure, if you were inclined to look at it, as a manager.

It all comes down to the individual and how you deal with it. I took it so personally. It made me feel a mixture of sadness and frustration. I could be out having dinner and find myself struggling to focus on anything except the worries and problems I had the next day; and that would be with me all the time. It borders on what I would imagine depression is like for people, and Karen would often ask me why I was putting myself through it.

I don't think managers do it because they enjoy the job. As Johnny Giles said to me soon after I was sacked by Newcastle, when we were working together on television in Dublin, 'It will take you a year to 18 months and then you will say to yourself, why did I ever do that job?'

He was right. It's like being a hamster on a wheel and you can't get off. I was perhaps lucky that because I had so much success as a player, I dropped straight into management at a high level. Being offered the job of player-manager of Rangers, I sort of fell into it, it wasn't something I ever planned to do, and then I got on that wheel and it was job after job and I never stood back to reflect.

The only time I did that was after I left Liverpool. I had about 15 months then before going to Galatasaray and I learnt in that period that I could live without it. I spent most of the next 12 months pottering around in the garden of my Cheshire home and I loved it. I married Karen in Las Vegas and I was able to completely leave the game behind me. I never went to matches and I didn't even watch them on television. I took myself entirely out of it all.

Karen was never into football, but would sometimes call out to the garden to tell me a certain game was on and I'd reply, 'So what?' It didn't mean anything to me anymore.

We also fitted in a holiday to Australia in this period, which got me thinking about buying a place there. We had dinner with Michael Parkinson and his wife one night and he sold the country to me, saying he spent about three months of every year there. The outdoor lifestyle and climate certainly appealed to me.

Yet most of my time was spent in my wellies in Cheshire, with a spade in my hand, or mowing the lawns. I'd go out after breakfast and could be quite content there all day, with only a break for a sandwich at lunchtime.

The days seemed to fly past and I didn't need anything else to keep my mind busy. I remained active and, as my back garden ran down to a lake, I had various grand ideas about what I was going to do with it.

It proved an excellent chance for me to take stock and recover from everything that happened at Liverpool and come to terms with the death of my father, which hit me hard, as losing my mother in my playing days had previously. Karen says that year out changed me as a person, that I started to listen more to other people's points of view.

I definitely became calmer and having Karen to confide in was a big part of that. I was no longer Mr Angry, the stereotype of me as a player and a manager. I had changed for the better, learnt from my many mistakes, and was no longer as restless. It had been straight into the Rangers job from playing, straight into the Liverpool job from Rangers and straight back into it after my operation, so I needed that year out before I took the Galatasaray job.

What made me go back? It was the excitement, I guess, of being offered the job. I didn't know much about Turkish football, other than they loved the game over there and I thought, 'Why not?' when I was offered a year's contract.

You get on that wheel, and every time you come off it, you get back on it again. After Galatasaray, I was immediately offered the Southampton job. Then I was offered the Torino job. That was followed by Benfica. When I came back from Portugal, I was almost immediately offered the Blackburn job, so I never had a period when I stood back, other than after I'd had my heart operation, left Liverpool and started to feel better and enjoy my life in a new house.

I don't think any manager does it because they wake up in the morning and think, 'This is a great job', unless you have just won a trophy, perhaps. Antonio Conte will feel like that just now, maybe.

What it came down to in the end for me was that the good times no longer compensated for when we lost games. The down after losing was far greater than the high of winning. What Johnny Giles said to me was 100 per cent correct. After 18 months, I thought,

'Christ, why did I do that?' The rewards are fabulous, but the price on the ticket for me became too great.

Taking some time out every so often, as I did after Liverpool, is the ideal for a manager, but it's not as easy as that if you analyse it. If you are successful, you will be offered a bigger job and a lot of people will take it because there's always someone having a bad time to offer an opportunity at a bigger club. If you are having a bad time and get sacked, you might want to take a few months out, but you also can't wait to get back and prove people wrong.

It's not a business where you can structure it and say I want to take a year out, because there's always a new kid on the block, always someone coming along. The only people who can do that are the real top men like Pep Guardiola, who took a sabbatical for a year after leaving Barcelona in 2012 before taking over at Bayern Munich.

The ones that get out on a high and leave their team as winners, like Fergie at Manchester United in 2013, are remembered for that, but they are rare exceptions to the rule.

HANDLE WITH CARE

The Premier League isn't perfect, but it's still the best, most-watched professional league in the world, televised in more than 200 countries, reaching more than 600 million homes and nearly five billion people. We have to manage our game very carefully going forward, if that popularity is to continue.

There are several aspects we need to be aware of. Firstly, we have to manage how it is perceived by the man in the street, so he isn't alienated from the players who play the game. Some do earn ridiculously big money these days, although there are a lot more who don't, but we need to take care of the game's image.

We also have to look after the next generation of supporters properly. They have to be the ones who follow on from their fathers and grandfathers to come and pay for the expensive season tickets and to generate the atmosphere at grounds up and down the country.

I definitely agree with the current campaigns to keep the costs of tickets down for the fans. When you break that down, if it means the players have to get the same money for two or three years, rather than a 25 per cent increase every other year, then that's fine. Do the players not get enough out of it already? It's time to think of the fans.

When it comes to my favourite ground to go to for atmosphere, I admit I am biased. Arsenal's stadium is fantastic in terms of modern facilities to work from, Old Trafford is aesthetically marvellous to look at, but my favourite is Anfield because it still generates the best atmosphere.

Not for every game, though. It's interesting now with the new Main Stand that you can see it emptying before half-time, and five minutes into the second half they have not come back from the executive suites, so that middle tier is still empty. That's something that was unimaginable going back a few years at Liverpool, and is another reminder that the bigger clubs can't forget the ordinary supporter in the rush to make extra money from their corporate guests.

We also need to be aware of the challenge from Spanish and German football. They would both like to have the number one league in the world, so we can't be complacent about the challenges out there in the rest of Europe and the rest of the world. The gloves are already off in this battle for global viewers, with La Liga kick-offs moving to increasingly earlier slots on Sunday mornings to attract bigger audiences in Asia.

When you break it down, if Barcelona, Real Madrid and Bayern Munich are better teams, why is the English league the best supported and most watched? It's because there is an element that makes it different and we must retain that.

The quality that separates us from them is that our football has always been a little bit more direct, a little bit more physical, played with a lot more passion. If it ain't broke, don't fix it, would be my advice on that score.

The Premier League referees have an enormous part to play in this. They cannot make it a sterile, non-tackling league, whatever the Fifa directives may say, otherwise we will just become like the rest. When I managed in Portugal, you would hear the referee's whistle every 10 seconds because of simulation, and that has crept into our game, too.

We have to retain our Britishness, which is a slightly more aggressive style of football, where there's a little bit more allowed to go on. Human beings like physical encounters. We like to see young fit men challenging each other physically, we don't want to make it bland and sterile, for it to become a chess game where you are making pretty but ineffective passing patterns in your own half.

It worries me that there are so many teams in the Premier League trying to play like Barcelona. Some games have become a bit of a five-a-side, a practice match. It's all about keeping possession and they are quite happy to do that in their own half.

I was at a Bournemouth–Swansea game towards the end of last season, where Bournemouth were looking over their shoulders, concerned with being dragged into the battle at the bottom, and Swansea were right in the relegation zone. Yet there was no ferocity in it, no real passion. We have to be careful there are not too many more games like that.

I'd like our game to remain a little bit more direct, a bit more fiery and explosive than that. I don't want it to become like Dutch football, where it is all just about technique and 30 to 40 passes in your own half. We have to guard against that. Keep possession by all means, but in the opposition's half, not your own where you are not under pressure.

One of the most common shouts you would have heard at Melwood, Liverpool's old training ground, from the late, great Ronnie Moran when we were playing small-sided games was to 'look forward' to the man in possession. Now, there's an obsession with midfielders dropping into the back four or back three and passing it 10 yards square.

An ex-England international midfielder, a contemporary of mine who was guilty of this, had this tendency christened after him at Liverpool and you would be compared to him if you were guilty of it. I discovered this in one of my first games for the club. I went into the back four, took a 10-yard pass off my left-back and then passed 10 yards to my centre-half. I was quite happy with that until I looked up and saw Ronnie and Joe Fagan screaming at me from the touch-line, waving at me to get up the pitch.

When I got in at half-time, they were waiting for me. 'Don't be doing that here, son, you got a pass off our left-back and passed it 10 yards to our centre-half and, by the way, our left-back, Emlyn Hughes, is the current England captain, don't you think he can pass it 20 yards for himself?' I never did it again.

We need to be careful we don't lose what has made our football different. It has always had an element of aggression and the reason for that is our public want it played that way. They might be prepared to accept a bit of chess match on the continent, but back home our fans have always demanded we play at a tempo and with a certain edge, perhaps because of our cooler climate.

There's an argument, which we contradicted in my time at Liverpool, that once you go into Europe, it's a different game. Well, we used to pass teams to death there, too, so we proved you can adapt. What we have to be careful of is becoming too safe and thinking it's all about possession. We need to have football that still gets you on the edge of your seat and is a bit more cut and thrust.

We can mix it up. We can still retain what we are good at, but we can also be good passing and possession teams going forward. Liverpool were the best out there in my time. Wherever we played, we had most of the ball. Rarely did we go anywhere in England or Europe where that wasn't the case.

I am not talking about becoming a Route One team. Wherever I have coached teams, that has not been my style, but I am fed up hearing about the Spanish way, the French way, the German way. There's no new and unique way of playing football. These countries, at a particular time, have each thrown up a fantastic group of players.

That's why France won the World Cup in 1998 then the European Championship in 2000, why Spain won the Euros in 2008, the World Cup in 2010 and then the Euros again in 2012. There's no new way of playing. It's just a nation produces a group of outstanding players and the system is tailored to them and they are successful. End of story. Yet you still get these halfwits who say we have to play like the Spanish, the Germans or the French. Really?

We need to remember what we are good at. Our league is a lot more competitive than theirs, for a start. What sort of league is the Bundesliga, when Bayern Munich, the biggest club, can repeatedly go and cherry-pick the best players from the second biggest club, Borussia Dortmund? How competitive is that?

Paris Saint-Germain have dominated in France, and Monaco have already begun dismantling the promising young team that won Ligue Un at their expense last season. Juventus have won Serie A for the last six seasons, and in La Liga, Atletico Madrid, who in 2014 broke the Barcelona–Real Madrid duopoly in Spain that lasted 9 seasons, are the exception that proves the rule there.

In England, you certainly wouldn't be putting your house on who is going to win the Premier League at the start of the season. We have had four different winners in the last five campaigns, although I see Leicester's incredible triumph of 2016 as a complete one-off that will never happen again. For all the big, fancy clubs to have such bad seasons simultaneously was a unique situation, but it's still an exceptionally competitive league.

Having played and managed abroad, I know from first-hand experience the big teams certainly get an easier ride there. The other teams don't really expect to beat them. They start off okay, but if they get a punch on the nose and lose an early goal, they don't have the same spirit to keep going. That's my experience of it, having managed big clubs in Italy, Turkey and Portugal, whereas our smaller clubs have that never-say-die attitude that's unique to British football and makes it so special.

Cristiano Ronaldo and Leo Messi play every game in La Liga, but most of the games are nowhere near as demanding as over here. They have it easier in Spain, they are not under the same pressure every week as our big clubs.

I'm not sure if that's healthy in the domestic context, but it helps them in Europe. Our clubs have not been good enough there in recent seasons and need to raise the standard in the years to come. Quite simply, there have been better teams around than ours, with key individuals that decide the big games.

Look at Cristiano Ronaldo's hat-trick for Real Madrid in the

Champions League semi-final against Atletico last sea

win it, if he's not playing? How many games has Leo Me

Barcelona through over the years?

Imagine taking those two players out and putting one at Manchester City over the last five years or one in at Chelsea. That would be enough to turn them into teams that could win the Champions League.

Spain's biggest clubs have dominated it because they have those two to call on. Players like Messi and Ronaldo don't come along in every generation. They are two great footballers who happen to be around at the same time, and I'll say it again that I don't expect to see anybody better than Messi, in particular, in my lifetime.

● ● ●

Television money has elevated the Premier League into the stratosphere in terms of spending power, creating some strange comparisons with other leagues. Rangers, my old club, get £2 million a year from television in Scotland. Sunderland, the bottom team in the Premier League last year, received almost £100 million.

It hurts me when I see teams like Bournemouth, where I go regularly, with gates of 11,000, and Rangers with over 40,000, yet I know Bournemouth could outbid Rangers every single day of the year for a player. That emphasises what television money has done for English football clubs like Bournemouth, who can flourish in the

Premier League with good management by Eddie Howe and his staff.

Personally, because I am Scottish and I know how big both clubs are, I think Rangers and Celtic would add to the interest in the Premier League enormously. The people who put money into the sport would have to dictate to the Premier League for it to happen, though.

The clubs would resist it because for many it would be a case of turkeys voting for Christmas, but nobody could deny that those two in the Premier League would create so much more interest on a worldwide scale, not just here in Britain.

I am not sure if people in England fully realise the size of those two clubs. Due to the demise of Scottish football, people think they have become smaller in some way, but they are absolute monsters. For it to happen, there would have to be a real downturn in the English Premier League for them to even contemplate it. That would be the last resort for them to reinvigorate and stimulate the interest again.

It's not just the Scottish clubs or those in other countries who are looking on enviously, but those big English clubs who have carelessly lost their status in the Premier League through mismanagement over the years. How do clubs like Aston Villa, Leeds United and Wolves feel, looking at Bournemouth in the Premier League?

Villa are a big football club. You realise that when you go there. We want clubs like that back in the Premier League, but there will always be big clubs not in it, because they haven't been managed correctly from the top. At least the soap opera that is Newcastle United has returned to the Premier League, which all adds to its attraction.

In general, club owners have to careful, though. The first thing they want to do is get their marquee manager in, a big name. It's like saying, 'Look who I have got as my manager', rather than going for the right person.

It's not just the foreign owners either. Successful British businessmen also become very wealthy and think, 'I'll buy a football club.' They are often entrepreneurs, who have been successful in several different fields, and make the mistake of thinking football is just another business. Football is not just another business.

You can have a business plan that gets you the league title one year, then you keep the same staff and business plan and are sitting in mid-table the following year. How is that possible? Because it's a bouncing ball that your fate lies with, you're also dealing with various personalities at any club, and you cannot make a business plan for that.

Then you make rash decisions, you fire the manager, and then it can be a snowball of mistakes. Look at Blackburn's demise as a case in point. What's paramount for any owner, foreign or British, is that they get a manager who understands that football club and understands the league they are in. Otherwise, they could spend years wasting money attempting to get it right.

The television riches mean our leading clubs have to pay over the odds for players in each transfer window, while we all sit watching the cumulative spend go higher and higher. Whenever Manchester United, Chelsea, Manchester City and, to a lesser extent, Arsenal, Liverpool and Tottenham, try to buy players on the continent, they are paying a vast premium.

That's because people know who owns the clubs, in the case of Roman Abramovich at Chelsea or Sheikh Mansour at City, or about United's wealth. It must irritate the life out of whoever does the deals at these clubs, that when they pick the phone up they know they are getting tickled and don't get any bargains.

Yet don't feel too sorry for these rich clubs, who can withstand a couple of barren years in terms of success and still spend heavily. Manchester United are no longer winning the Premier League, but their money from television and commercial operations still allowed them to go and break the world transfer record for Paul Pogba despite not being in the Champions League. That's the financial power they have now.

Manchester City are a different story again. They are arguably the richest club in the world, along with Paris Saint-Germain. Their owners are so wealthy they could buy every other club in the Premier League, including Chelsea and United, if they wanted to and were allowed to. That level of funding will continue as long as the people in the Middle East retain their interest. You have to give them great credit, because it has not just been about the fur coat, they have built a superb infrastructure in east Manchester, too. The easiest way, if it had just been about fame and glory, would have been to spend the money only on the players on the pitch. City, though, have not only spent big on players, they have also invested money in what was a run-down area of Manchester.

The other clubs can't compete with City financially, but no-one is going to feel sorry for Arsenal or Liverpool or any of the rest of that super-group in the top six, when they can go out and spend £100 million every close season. It's also about clever recruitment. Look at Luis Suarez, the best of his type around. Liverpool didn't pay big bucks for him – £23 million from Ajax proved to be excellent value when they sold him to Barcelona for £65 million. If you can cherry-pick the right players, you have a chance to win the league.

Tottenham sold Gareth Bale for £86 million to Real Madrid in 2013 and more or less wasted all of that, except for Christian Eriksen at £12 million from Ajax, on the players they brought in, but they have done better since with Dele Alli and Harry Kane emerging. I hope my old club continue to grow at their new stadium and that they can overcome the mental block they seemed to have at first, which I don't get, about playing at Wembley. That seed would have been firmly planted in some of the weaker personalities' heads. That's when your big men have to stand up and drag those lesser lights through that mental block, but everything else is rosy in their garden, when you look at the average age of their squad.

It will help them that they are a London team. Big players today want to come to London, because of what's on offer away from the football, and they have the money to be able to enjoy all that in a big city. When I was a player, you didn't want to go to London, simply because it was too expensive to live there. You certainly couldn't go shopping at Harrods every day of the week or out to the restaurants in Knightsbridge, but it's a different world for players today.

That's an advantage the London clubs have and it is being driven by the money the players earn now. Not only can they afford the best, there's also an element of anonymity: you can get lost in London, where maybe you can't in the provincial cities. That also makes London more attractive to modern footballers.

That could also work in West Ham's favour if they settle in at the London Stadium. They and Everton, who are also moving to a new stadium, will think with a fair wind behind them they can maybe break into that top six.

It's not impossible, but their chances of doing so are slim, because of the kind of money that these big clubs have now with their commercial operations, which gives them the most ridiculous spending power. Do I see the other clubs making that jump on a consistent basis? No. They will continue to be just outside that elite group.

I don't believe there's a possibility of another Leicester unless someone comes along, like the Manchester City owners, and has a right go at it. It could be they are attracted to the club or went to university in that city and fell in love with it, or whatever, so they buy the club and spend their fortune on it.

Jack Walker did it at Blackburn, when the money and the stakes were quite different, and Manchester United, Liverpool, Chelsea and Arsenal couldn't compete. People all round the world know where Hull is now, where Bournemouth is, where Blackburn is. The football club can put relatively unknown places in England on the map. It's great for these cities. They get a buzz from it.

It's a global game now, it's not about the local butcher owning the football club anymore and making all the decisions. They are made by expensively-hired chief executives, from all walks of life, and the foreign owners. The world is a very small place today.

Yet foreign owners and the money involved can also be destabilising for managers. We used to laugh at the Latin way of changing managers after a few bad results. I got six games at Torino, so I witnessed that at first hand. We're not there yet, but we'll get there because of more foreign owners with their standards coming to our football.

It's hard to be critical of Chelsea, for example, because of the amount of trophies they have won by constantly changing their managers, although they have also thrown enormous sums of money at it. Look at the situation of Watford changing their manager every season, which goes against the grain of continuity, but they are surviving in the Premier League on it. Ultimately, though, because they are not big spenders, that will come back to bite them on the backside. In many cases now, we are playing by European standards in our impatience for success.

Foreign is fashionable in the Premier League, for managers and players, but that doesn't mean that everyone who comes is a brilliant addition to our football. For example, who decided that Bob Bradley, an American, would be a good choice to bring in at Swansea last season when he had no experience of British football, was inheriting a team that were in the bottom three and had managed a second division team in France previously? Similarly, who thought bringing Remi Garde from France into Aston Villa the previous season was a good idea when they were fighting against relegation?

It might take three months for them to come in, get their feet under the table and understand the English game, and by then you could already be down. You've brought in someone who doesn't know the squad he's inheriting, the teams he's playing against and doesn't know the ferocity of our league. I just don't get it.

I'd like to see more former players involved in the decision-making process at their old clubs, to stop those strange calls being made. The German clubs do that better than anybody, keeping a non-executive footballing board if you like, including some ex-players. Not all of them are equipped for it, of course, but many are and it would stop some of the more bewildering decisions we witness.

As for the influx of foreign players, again they have brought some good things to the table and some bad things. There was very little simulation in our game until 15 to 20 years ago, for example, but I think finally the British player said, 'We can't beat them, so we'll join them', and now they all do it. Some of the great players that have arrived in the Premier League have definitely added to our game, but for every one of them, there have also been 30 or 40 average ones.

For community clubs, like Bournemouth and Swansea, it's just about survival, that's all you can hope for. There is a league of six at the top and another league of 14 beneath, maybe give or take Everton who are rarely in the relegation battle.

All you can do in that league of 14 is get yourself a fabulous stadium and training ground and get on a sound financial footing, where you could survive the doomsday scenario of getting relegated. You also get a youth programme in place, where you start to develop some of your own players.

You do need a bit of luck in terms of recruitment, and you can also have a bit of a golden period with the players who come through the youth development system. That's two large slices of good fortune you are looking for when you are building a team on a smaller budget compared to the big boys.

There's no magic formula in youth development, though. I go back to the Class of '92. If Manchester United had found the Holy Grail, it would have been repeated every other year, but it has never happened again for them since.

It's the same as certain nations having golden periods in producing players. That was United's. They got a load of very good kids through at the same time, who became major players for a long period in their first team.

Southampton, near where I live now, have enjoyed a good period of late. They have produced some very good kids, but that won't go on forever either. They won't keep producing kids like Gareth Bale and those who have followed him into their first team since. It's a bonus if you bring a player through at a Premier League club, rather than buying one the manager can really rely on, but there's no guarantee of it.

● ● ●

I reckon three relegation places is the right amount for the Premier League. It generates an excitement at the bottom as well, not just at the top. The games down there can often have more riding on them towards the end of each season, and the TV coverage often responds to that in the closing weeks.

The real prospect of relegation adds a competitive edge to the Premier League, and it gives us more games that mean something each season. Any attempts to create a closed shop, where clubs cannot be punished for failing to perform, should be resisted.

Some things will change, though. I reckon it's inevitable, and will happen fairly soon, that clubs are going to have to go abroad and play some Premier League games, probably in Asia. Ultimately, that will happen, like the NFL bringing their American Football fixtures to London as they look for new markets.

It has to, when you think about it logically. To maintain the interest in those countries, and it is enormous, it is a natural follow-on to have live games there that are televised back in Britain, rather than the other way round. The players could jump on a plane on a Tuesday or Wednesday, fly 10 hours, play the game and come back straight afterwards. They will all be in first class or business class with whatever they need.

That's going to happen and, again, will only bring more wealth to the Premier League. The clubs are looking to create as much interest as possible in these countries with enormous populations; that's why so many have already been there on pre-season tours. So I see that as a natural progression: that Premier League clubs will go and play competitive games in different parts of the world during a season.

It's very much in their interests to do that. It's true they have to get that past their own supporters, but they will argue that if they want to see them buy the very best players and come to the best stadiums, it is part of the deal – two, maybe three big games played abroad every year.

I know the Italian clubs are keen on a European league because their football is on its backside. That's why they want to change it to playing European games at weekends and domestic ones in midweek. Our league is brimming, all the money is in it, so of course every other league that's not doing so well will want to fill their stadiums and get more lucrative TV deals, too.

When Milan and Inter were flying, they wanted a Champions League because of the guaranteed three home games at the group stage, but that's old hat now because it's not about guaranteed income from three home games, it's about television money. Right now, there's no indication that people on the other side of the world want to see us playing more European games. They want more of the English Premier League and we have to be careful to keep it that way.

There's also no doubt the game has evolved and people are more mercenary now and it's harder to build sides and keep them together until the time is right to break them up. I saw a sign of that when I moved to Italy with Sampdoria. Gianluca Vialli was from Cremona, Roberto Mancini was from Bologna. They didn't buy houses when they came to Genoa, they just rented them.

That was the Italian way. You bought a place where you were from and just rented where you played. In England, you bought a house, another house and then another. You put down roots at each club. In Italy, it was more like, 'I'm not getting too involved in what goes on in this city, I'm not going to be part of the community for long.' For the majority, that's how it was.

It was more of a professional view of it and that's what we have here now, too. Few of the foreign players buy houses here. If they come in with that attitude, 'I'm here for a couple of years, then I'm off', how can you ever recreate that togetherness we had at Liverpool, or that United had?

The British lads, who want to be like that, instead end up being like the foreign players. It has rubbed off on them, too. That culture then becomes the norm. How are you going to build a proper football club? How can there be another lasting dynasty like Liverpool's, like United's?

The Liverpool teams I played in were largely British and Irish, whereas now the Premier League squads are drawn from all around the world. That's globalisation, the increased movement of people between countries and continents, and it's a follow-on from what's happening in society.

One thing I experienced as a player in Italy that I wouldn't be keen on being introduced here is a winter break. Our winter is not that severe and it's also part of our culture to play at that time of year. We talk about being tired, but with the amount of money the clubs have today, they can build and pay a squad that can withstand that hectic festive period. I liked to play football, so it was an unnecessary break in the routine as far as I was concerned.

Serie A was the home of the superstars when I played there. Zico, Diego Maradona and Michel Platini were all there during my two years at Sampdoria, but the Premier League has greater status now. We perhaps don't have the very top players, who end up at Barcelona, Real Madrid and Bayern Munich, but we can attract the next level below that. We don't lose out to anybody else really.

As a player, if you had a chance to go to Juventus, or you could play for either Manchester United, Liverpool, Chelsea or Manchester City, you would probably choose the English Premier League. If you are a Latin, Spain's an enormous attraction. If you are northern European, maybe it's Bayern Munich, or Manchester United, Manchester City or Chelsea these days.

When I went to Liverpool in 1978, they were so dominant at

that time that if I'd also had chance to go to Real Madrid, I would still have ended up at Anfield. That was their pull back then. Now, Liverpool are just hanging on to their place among England's elite. With that tremendous history, they will always be able to attract very good players, but will they be able to attract the very best? I'm not so sure.

Being in the Champions League again will help, but I still don't think Liverpool will suddenly go out and break the world transfer record. I don't think Jurgen Klopp wants to work that way and the people who own the club and make the decisions don't want to work that way either.

Nobody wants to work that way, ideally. Ed Woodward, Manchester United's executive vice-chairman, doesn't. He'd rather be buying players that are about to explode onto the scene than paying a premium for the established stars. United have paid way over the odds in the last couple of transfer windows, but that's the price on the ticket of being Manchester United. What's the alternative? There isn't one.

We have seen it at City, too, with John Stones at £50 million and Kevin de Bruyne at £55 million. There's no alternative, other than don't compete for them and just bring players through your youth development squad gradually.

Manchester United paid £89 million for Pogba. He's a long way from being world-class, a long way from being the best in his position. Will he get there? We'll see, but £100 million players in the Premier

League will become the norm if the spending by the big clubs continues on the same course.

● ● ●

So many great players have been brought into our league, and I have the privilege of watching them on a weekly basis through my television work and enjoying the surrounding stories unfold over the course of a season.

When Chelsea won the Premier League in Antonio Conte's first season, I was on the pitch after they were presented with the trophy and even interviewed a few of the players who had taken them to the title. I found Diego Costa a particularly entertaining watch. He's a character. Someone you would love to have as a teammate, but wouldn't enjoy playing against very much. He looks like the bad guy that Clint Eastwood comes up against in one of the spaghetti westerns from the 1960s and 70s.

Eden Hazard gets you on the edge of your seat, with his dribbling ability and exciting runs, but goes to ground far too easily. I admire N'Golo Kante for his style of perpetual motion, in and around people all the time. Kante and Nemanja Matic (now at Manchester United) are a good pair of modern-day midfielders, while Pedro brings industry as well as skill to his work on the wing.

Gary Cahill, who was always a very solid citizen, has got better and better as his career has gone on and emerged as a leader at

Chelsea, while David Luiz was a revelation when they won the title because he was in the central position of the three defenders, and if he made a mistake there it would end up with a shot at Chelsea's goal. He was far more disciplined as a result I felt, and what about Cesar Azpilicueta? The Spanish defender was a model of consistency and played every minute of every league match on the way to the title.

We have some great goalkeepers in the Premier League. Thibaut Courtois is one, so are Hugo Lloris, David de Gea and Petr Cech. At the other end of the pitch, I like Sergio Aguero and Gabriel Jesus, who looks another goalscorer on the early evidence, at Manchester City. De Bruyne's not consistent enough, but there's a world-class player in there. I also love watching David Silva for his creative talent. Eriksen, Kane and Alli at Tottenham and Philippe Coutinho at Liverpool are players at my former clubs that excite me whenever I watch them.

Antonio Conte reminded us last season that you play a system because it suits your players, not the other way round. The 3–4–3 that Chelsea's manager used so well also suits Tottenham because of their personnel. The modern full-back's priority seems to be to get forward and create, as opposed to defending, and Danny Rose has been as good as anyone at that. Eric Dier could drop back beside Toby Alderweireld – who, along with Cahill, is the best central defender in the Premier League for me – and Jan Vertonghen to also create a 3–4–3 for Mauricio Pochettino's side.

Systems come in and out of fashion, but the key is finding one that works for the players you have. Sometimes you can get too obsessed with what the opposition are doing. At Liverpool, we played against teams that tried every formation against us, but we still beat them because we had our own tried and trusted way of playing that we knew worked for us.

Conte's success has raised the stakes for the other so-called super-managers. Pep Guardiola and Jose Mourinho have had a couple of transfer windows under their belts now at the Manchester clubs and the pressure is on. They arrived with so much goodwill because of what they had done previously in the game, but they will be under much more scrutiny from now on. Guardiola's first year in England may also have been a wake-up call to him that there is no new way of playing football.

Jurgen Klopp's had his honeymoon period as well at Liverpool. That's the pressure you face when you are a big football club, with owners and supporters who demand success because they are used to it.

It's not all bad news, because the contracts these managers are on are heavily weighted in their favour. If you are a manager of that standing, it's not the end of the world if you are shown the door. You can always get another job.

There are so many different dynamics at the big clubs and we get to live it because of the media interest, the 24-hour rolling news on the television, social media, and so on. We get it in real time, which makes it all the more fascinating.

Each season throws up fresh talking points and I still find myself excited on the eve of a new one. As I said at the start of this book, it has been an absolute privilege to be involved in the game as a player, manager and now in television. Since I was aged 15, these past 50 years in football have simply flown by for me, and I'm looking forward to the next few years . . . as long as we take good care of our fabulous game.

ACKNOWLEDGEMENTS

Graeme Souness

I would like to thank Douglas Alexander for his professionalism and uncanny ability to 'get' me.

Douglas Alexander

Thanks to Graeme for asking me to help with this book, to Jonathan Taylor at Headline for making it happen, and also to Fahri Ecvet, Lily Phillips and Tim Ruppersbery at Wasserman for their assistance.

Alex Butler and Nick Greenslade at *The Sunday Times* sports desk in London have been extremely supportive of Graeme's column since it started in 2013, while Jason Allardyce, Mark MacAskill, and Mark Palmer in Glasgow are all excellent colleagues to share an office with.

My late father, Douglas, was a wonderful dad to me, while Christine, my mum, Craig, my brother, and Lynsey, my sister, have all kept me going with their kindness and wisdom over the last year.

Above all, love to David, the best wee boy a dad could wish for, and to Karen, for making life so much brighter than it would have been.

PICTURE CREDITS

Rex by Shutterstock: p.1 top (Owen Barnes/Associated Newspapers); p.2 top (Associated Newspapers); p.2 middle (Colorsport); p.4 middle (Colorsport); p.5 top right (Colorsport); p.7 middle (Colorsport); p.8 top (Colorsport); p.8 bottom (Colorsport); p.9 bottom right (Andrew Kiggins/Daily Mail); p.12 top (Colorsport); p.12 middle (Colorsport); p.12 bottom (Imago/Germany); p.13 top (Ted Blackbrow/Daily Mail); p.13 bottom (Andy Hooper/Daily Mail); p.14 bottom right (David Ashdown/The Independent); p.16 bottom (Kieran McManus/BPI)

Mirrorpix: p.1 bottom; p.3 bottom; p.4 bottom; p.5 bottom; p.6 top; p.11 middle

Getty Images: p.2 bottom (Rob Taggart/Central Press); p.3 top (Mike

Brett/Popperfoto); p.3 middle (Allsport UK); p.4 top (Bob Thomas); p.5 top left (Bob Thomas); p.6 middle (Bob Thomas); p.7 top (David Cannon); p.7 bottom (Bob Thomas); p.14 bottom left (Gary M Prior); p.16 top (Ben Radford/Visionhaus)

Press Association Images: p.6 bottom (SMG); p.9 top (SMG); p.9 bottom left (SMG); p.10 top; p.10 bottom (Rangers FC); p.11 top (EMPICS Sport); p.11 bottom (Phil O'Brien/EMPICS Sport); p.13 middle (Matthew Ashton/EMPICS Sport); p.14 top (Phil Noble); p.15 bottom left (John Walton/EMPICS Sport); p.15 bottom right (John Giles)

Reuters Media Express: p.15 top (Lee Smith Livepic)

INDEX